# The Music
of Creation

*The Lessons of St. Francis*

*Meditations from Solitude*

*The Master Musician*

*Passion for God* (VOL. 3 OF THE REFLECTION SERIES)

*Blessings*

*Simplicity* (with Dan O'Neill)

*Hermitage*

*Reflections on the Gospels*, VOL. 1

*Reflections on the Gospels*, VOL. 2

*The Lover and the Beloved: A Way of Franciscan Prayer*

*Fire of God*

*Changes*

JEREMY P. TARCHER/PUTNAM

*a member of*
*Penguin Putnam Inc.*
*New York*

*The*
# Music
*of*
# Creation

*Foundations*
*of a*
*Christian Life*

# John Michael
# Talbot

WITH STEVE RABEY

Most Tarcher/Putnam books are available at special quantity discounts for bulk purchases for sales promotions, premiums, fund-raising, and educational needs. Special books or book excerpts also can be created to fit specific needs. For details, write Putnam Special Markets, 375 Hudson Street, New York, NY 10014.

Jeremy P. Tarcher/Putnam
a member of
Penguin Putnam Inc.
375 Hudson Street
New York, NY 10014
www.penguinputnam.com

Library of Congress Cataloging-in-Publication Data

Talbot, John Michael.
The music of creation: foundations of a Christian Life / John Michael Talbot.
p.   cm.
ISBN 0-87477-983-9
1. Catholic Church—Doctrines.   2. Spirituality—Catholic Church.
I. Title.
BX1754.T34 1999
230'.2—dc21                    99-15574   CIP

Printed in the United States of America
1   3   5   7   9   10   8   6   4   2
This book is printed on acid-free paper. ♾

BOOK DESIGN BY DEBORAH KERNER

# Acknowledgments

Archbishop Bernard Cardinal Law of Boston,
who helped me along the way of patristic thought.

My spiritual father, Fr. Martin Wolter, O.F.M.

Fr. Alan McCoy, O.F.M., who taught me
how to apply contemporary thought.

Huston Smith, who introduced me to religion.

And Steve Rabey, who should receive a special thanks
for helping me to commit my thoughts to paper.

IN MEMORY OF MY MOTHER,

JAMIE TALBOT

# Contents

# The Music
## of Creation

# Introduction

THINGS MUST HAVE A BEGINNING, SO I WILL BEGIN, AS ALL things do, with God.

God exists. "I AM" was his revelation to Moses. Called by different names and concepts in different languages, cultures, and religions, God is the Reality through, with, in, and beyond all reality.

Each one of us is conceived in our mother's womb by God through our parents. God has a beautiful plan and potential for each one of us. It is filled with love, truth, goodness, justice, and mercy. It is simple, innocent, and pure. Deep down inside, we know that this is the real us, the real me, the real you.

Humanity seeks this reality. It is the Tao—or Way—for Taoists and Confucianists. It is the self and spirit for Hindus. It is the original child of God.

But almost as soon as we're born, we begin to conceal that child.

All faiths teach that we live in a world where the picture is out of focus. Something has gone dreadfully wrong. And as children of God born into a world out of kilter, we begin to acclimate ourselves to this environment.

God's plan for our beauty and innocence begins to grow dim and hard to see, and we feel strangely out of place. As we enter primary school, we've already learned the first lessons about how to cover up the traces of this original child. By the time we're teenagers, many of us have become quite accomplished at concealing this true identity. As adults, we have almost entirely obscured our original self. Sadly, most of us have become numbed to the fact that a child of God is even there!

Jesus tells us we must become children to enter the kingdom of God. Jesus, who is a unique manifestation of the "I AM" God, shows us a way to rediscover that original child of God and to let that child be "born again." Jesus calls us back to that pristine innocence and purity. He calls us back to the way of love, joy, peace, faith, hope, and charity. This is the way we all long for deep within. It is the way of God. We are children of God who have been created to seek these things of goodness and beauty, and we are unhappy and frustrated within and without until we find them.

Jesus shows us the way home. He shows the child how to be reborn. He is the doorway. In the Gospel of John, Jesus expresses it like this: "I am the way and the truth and the life."

In order for this child to be born again, the false and illusory self must die and fall away. We must let go of that self entirely, holding nothing back. Only then can we rest from the labor of sustaining our delusions, and be at peace and truly free.

The process of renouncing this false self and embracing our true self in God is a lifelong journey, and it is this journey that is the focus of this book.

God simply IS. He is I AM.

## ENTERING THE CAVE OF THE HEART

FOR CENTURIES, mystics, prophets, and contemplatives of every major religious tradition have been called to the solitude and silence of the "cave of the heart" before they embarked on their mission to the world.

Jesus, too, withdrew to the desert, and from there he foretold that some of his followers would migrate to the mountains and caves of Judea in the midst of the troubles and agitations of the world. Later, Christian monks found refuge in those same caves along the wadis—or dried riverbeds—of the Judean desert in the early centuries of the Christian monastic movement. Today, monks continue to dwell within caves, living lives of solitude and silence throughout every region of the world.

We too are called to the "cave of the heart" in the midst of our own modern lives. We may be solitary monks, church ministers, or active business people involved in the hustle and bustle of the modern city. Regardless of who we are or what we do, we are all called to make the journey inward so we can rediscover the spiritual focus that reorders and harmonizes all the other aspects of our emotional, mental, and physical lives. We must rediscover the primacy of the spirit so that the thoughts and images of the soul and the emotions and the senses of the body can be put back into proper harmony.

*The Music of Creation* is an exploration of this inward voyage of discovery, which prepares us to go back outward and forward to bring goodness and love to all creation. It is about the rediscovery of spirit so that soul and body can find their proper and most harmonious relationship.

## CATHOLIC

MY PILGRIMAGE has led me to an ancient and enduring expression of the Christian faith. I live and write as a Catholic Christian. The word "catholic" means "universal and full." In the words of one of the creeds of the Catholic Church, being universal and full means believing what Christians have "believed universally from the beginning."

I am not a theologian. Nor am I a bishop, or even a high-ranking church adviser. I am a simple lay monk and the founder of a rather obscure new monastic community in an obscure part of an obscure state nestled high in a quiet valley in the Ozark Mountains.

My definition of "catholic" is more personal, and more pastoral. For me, to be a Catholic Christian means letting Jesus take control of my entire life, universally and fully. I give God my body, my soul, and my spirit. I am reminded of the prayer of Charles de Foucauld: "I abandon myself to you." Saint Ignatius of Loyola expressed the same desire in his prayer: "I surrender it all to Jesus." I set this prayer of Saint Ignatius to music in the song "Surrender" on my *Hiding Place* recording:

*I surrender it all to Jesus*
*I surrender it all to God's will*
*I surrender it all for the Kingdom of God*
*I surrender my life, my all.*

What this surrender means is that I give God my actions, my words, my emotions, and my thoughts. I pray that these things may be brought into full harmony with the beautiful, eternal music of God, so that my spirit may be born again in his Spirit. When I am surrendered to God in this way, I can simply intuit the things of God without worrying or striving. This does not mean that I am involved in some solitary, pioneering, esoteric search. Rather, I plumb the depths of the full sacramental and devotional traditions of the Catholic Christian faith as it has always been taught by the fathers and theologians of the Church.

As I surrender my life to God, I lay down anything in my life that creates discord with God's mystical harmony. I release my own habitually disordered behaviors, yield control of my powerful emotions, let go of my runaway passions and desires, and renounce my negative and harmful attitudes. On a deeper level, I submit my innermost spirit to God's gentle guiding, making myself vulnerable to his all-freeing love, joy, and peace. In the process, I rediscover the beauty and innocence God had originally planned for me when I was first conceived in my mother's womb.

It is this inner enlightenment that we all long for. It is this child of God that longs and waits to be reborn. But it cannot be reborn until the old, false self passes away and dies. Until this happens, we are at war within, as Paul expressed so clearly: "What I do, I do not understand. For I do not do what I want, but I do what I hate."

As long as this old self persists, it will prevail. We must totally, thoroughly, and "universally" let it go. Only then can we be reborn.

Of course, the old self will try to regain the upper hand. But once we have made the choice to submit to God with an authentic act of the will, the deed is done, the process has begun. There is no turning back. All that awaits is to surrender more fully to Jesus in every aspect of our lives, submitting ever fiber of our being—even the hidden recesses of the soul—to his control.

Just as Jesus died on a cross, we must ourselves take up the cross, laying down our old self to make way for the new. The cross is the way, the truth, and the life of Jesus. The cross is the paradox of paradoxes that unlocks the mystery of mysteries. The cross erases the separation between God and humanity and creation, allowing us to experience oneness with God.

Through the cross, we find new life in death. And as we experience new life from God, we begin to know mystically many other paradoxes of the Christian life, finding wisdom in folly, riches in poverty, freedom in slavery, profound communication in deepest silence, eternal companionship in solitude, knowledge in unknowing, eternal light in darkness, and unimagined riches in spiritual poverty.

This union with God takes us beyond contradiction and duality into the coincidence of opposites, where all is made one in God through Christ. As we are awakened, every emotion and every thought, and every sense of sight, smell, sound, touch, and taste can become a breakthrough from the eternal to the now, and from the now to eternity. There is nothing more but to "be" with God, the eternal I AM.

Have you ever sensed God calling you through the mysterious inner workings of his Spirit? Embracing this call will take you on the adventure of a lifetime, and will help you rediscover your original godly conception and eternal destiny as a human being. Regardless of your personal history or spiritual tradition, I humbly invite you to know the deeper reality of this catholic, universal, and full life in Jesus.

## THE CALL TO COMMUNITY

GOD CALLS OUT to each one of us individually, but the spiritual journey is not a solitary affair. There is a corporate, or communal, dimension to being a Catholic Christian.

We all live in God's creation, where both human and nonhuman beings dwell in communal societies. Humans call their groupings packs, or tribes, or cities, or countries, or empires. Many animals live and work together as well. Wolves run in packs. Cattle and sheep congregate in herds. Fish swim in schools. From the smallest insects to the largest elephants, most of the creatures in God's creation are communal beings.

The Church is the Christian community. In the words of the Creed, there is one holy, catholic, and apostolic Church. I have never found so complete a unity anywhere else on earth as I have in the Catholic Church. Other churches and religions have wonderful gifts from God, but I have never found any other institution that possesses so many of these gifts in one place, even though we don't always use God's gifts as we should, and we have kept many of them on the back shelf of the spiritual pantry, where they remain out of reach and have little practical benefit.

Though we believe that God, in his perfection, guides us in all areas of our faith, the Catholic Church isn't perfect, and Catholic Christians greatly respect, honor, and love other churches and religions for the gifts they possess and use in wonderful ways. In dialogue with members of these other churches and faiths, we humbly learn from them as brother and sister believers. We also are challenged by witnessing the ways they utilize the particular gifts God has given to them. For example, Vatican Council II (1962–65) commended evangelical Christians' emphasis on the Word of God. In a similar manner, the Church has praised Pentecostals for their emphasis on the work of the Spirit.

Most important, we recognize that we do not possess the gifts in and of ourselves. They are gifts of God. They are always to be used with humble respect and reverence. This attitude keeps us from self-righteousness and pride, from frustration and anger. We are merely stewards of the gifts God gives us. They belong to all people in God.

I could list dozens of the beautiful gifts that I see at work in the Catholic Church. Instead, here are four that I appreciate the most:

- The Church has a *contemplative and mystical heritage* that is deep and broad, and which integrates Eastern and Western approaches to prayer.
- There are millions of *Pentecostals or charismatics* in the world, but the largest single and united body of these enthusiastic believers is in the Catholic Church.
- The Church has ancient *monastic traditions*. Through the centuries, there has been a great flowering of monastic Christianity, and this flowering manifests itself in a wide variety of consecrated communities, where people's lifestyles are based on radical (yet not fanatical) dedication to poverty, chastity, and obedience.
- The Church's strong, gentle commitment to *peace and justice*, which is based on its deep reverence for human life, has tangibly changed unjust social structures around the globe.

In the Church, I have found an institution that is ancient without being irrelevant, progressive without being trendy, committed to Scriptural fundamentals without being fundamentalist, and traditional without being archconservative.

And while some see the Church as huge and immovable, history has witnessed its willingness to allow experimentation, its graciousness in allowing people to follow God, and its openness to genuine renewal and even reform in every era and generation. Something so universal and full—something so catholic—must be from our universal and full God.

The Church faces many difficulties. When I was becoming a Catholic, I was concerned about some of these problems. My spiritual father showed me that for the past twenty centuries, the Church has walked first on one foot, then on the other, first left, then right, but seen in perspective has walked in a relatively straight line on its journey from the time of Christ to our own present day. In the short term, it may look as if the Church is confused, or changing directions. But when viewed in the long term, she moves steadily and surely toward her goal on her journey homeward.

## HESYCHIA

THE SPIRITUAL JOURNEY is a communal one, but much of our inner growth comes through personal and private communion with God. The monks of the Christian Orthodox East use the Greek word *hesychia* to describe the stillness and silence of their unique way of life, a life that is specially crafted to nurture and accommodate contemplative prayer and mystical union with God.

Though many people today are fascinated by monks and mystics, few of us follow their example by making room for stillness and silence in our hectic daily lives. Perhaps the wisdom of these Eastern monks can help us understand the beauty of their spiritual practices, and help us find practical ways to apply their insight to our spiritually thirsty lives.

One image the monks use to describe hesychia is that of a pond. When a pond is agitated, it becomes muddy and unclear. You cannot see what is within, nor does it reflect what is without. But as the pond becomes still, the water settles and slowly clarifies. When the water is still and clear, you can see the reality of what is within. Its surface also becomes mirror-like, reflecting all that is without and providing a brilliant display of the surrounding trees and foliage, the animals and people along its bank, as well as the very blue of the endless sky.

Our souls are similar. Most of us lead lives that have become turbulent and agitated through worldly concerns and anxieties, rather than lives of calmness, stillness, and union with God's harmony and peaceful plan. Consequently, we cannot even see the reality of our own soul, our deepest essence. Our agitation causes us to be confused by many of our own thoughts and emotions, and by our normal habitual behavior of daily life.

Hesychia is a way of stillness that helps calm the waters of the soul, bringing us inner peace. Once that occurs, we can see underneath the turbulent surface of our lives, perhaps for the first time. In hesychia, our spirit, soul, and body become mirrors reflecting the reality of God and the original harmony and peace he intended for all creation.

Achieving this kind of clarity is only the beginning of a lifelong process, because once we can see into the pond of our soul, we can begin to make out some of the old garbage that has lain on the bottom for many years without detection. When we first see this garbage, we reach in to remove it. This will temporarily disturb the waters again, but after another period of hesychia, we can look once again into a still, clear pond. Except that now the pond will be cleaner, and more able to reflect clearly the glorious beauty of God and all creation.

There's another image the monks use to describe the soul stillness they devote their lives to achieving. It is that of the spider. After the spider has created its beautiful, symmetrical web, it stays absolutely quiet and still so that it can sense the slightest motion of the web. For the spider, movement on the web means that lunch is served! After a bug lands in his snare, the spider can be nourished.

For us, movement doesn't mean mealtime. Instead, the image of the spider shows us how we can enter into a life of hesychia, or still-ness, so that we can perceive even the slightest movement in our soul. That movement may be good or bad, the promptings of God's grace or the enemy's temptation or distraction. Regardless, our still-ness makes us aware of movement, and then we may respond accordingly. As a result, each moment and every movement becomes a new opportunity to respond in God's way. Every encounter becomes a chance for growth and for responding to the leadings of the soul.

Unfortunately, most of us are so busy with the superficial things of life that we never peer beneath the surface to see the movement down within our souls. We are oblivious to this deeper activity. We are soul-dead.

The only remedy is hesychia, which brings watchfulness and attentiveness, sensitizes us to the leading of God's Spirit, and alerts us to our plentiful opportunities for deeper spiritual growth.

## REMAKING OUR LIVES

WHEN JESUS first began to preach, his urgent message to the world was simple and direct: "Repent, for the kingdom of heaven is at hand!"

The kingdom of heaven is at hand for us too, right here and right now. God is waiting for us to welcome him, so that he might break through to every soul, and so that every soul might break through to him. By reaching out to God as he is reaching out to us, our spirits will break through the limits of physicality to live in the Spirit even in the midst of the now. Our bodies and souls—along with our actions, emotions, and thoughts—will remain in the con-creteness of time and space, but our spirits will be in eternity and infinity already through our union with God's Spirit.

We all experience brief instances of such breakthroughs already:

while taking a walk in the woods and observing the luxuriant beauty of creation; while listening to a piece of fine music and experiencing the beauty of human creativity; or while doing something as simple as enjoying a conversation with others, and marveling as our souls become united together. Such experiences, brief and fleeting as they may be, are the beginnings of breakthroughs to eternity and infinity through the common elements of everyday life.

For me, such breakthroughs to eternity often happen in prayer. It's as if I am suddenly transported beyond words and concepts to an experience where the light goes on. For me, such breakthroughs encompass the mystical high points of life, the more mundane, ordinary events, and everything in between. Sometimes, a breakthrough can be as simple as me praying, "Today is a beautiful day, and I see Jesus in this." On another day, I may pray, "Today's going to be a real struggle, and I can see Jesus in this."

Through regular prayer, our lives become enlightened and reformed. This does not mean we do not continue to face real difficulties, challenges, and trials. These too are reality. But as we grow spiritually, such challenges take on a whole new meaning, and even contribute to our growth if we allow them to.

This ongoing spiritual reformation is what Jesus calls us to, and it's what we were created to experience. To be reformed means to be formed again. It is like we are all clay pots, but unfortunately we are all flawed and incomplete. Our pots are cracked. Cracks can be anything the Bible describes as sin, from little stuff like anger, frustration, irritability, and anxiety to big stuff like adultery and murder. You could say we are a bunch of "crack pots."

How should we fix these cracks? Do we fill them with glue while leaving the rest of our pot untouched? This is how many of us deal with the weak and damaged portions of our lives. We say, "Just fix the problem, but leave the rest of me alone." Such superficial mending jobs don't really get at the underlying problems. They merely conceal the deeper damage, postponing an inevitable breakage.

Experienced potters take a more serious approach. They begin by soaking a damaged pot in water. After sufficient soaking, the pot becomes clay again, and the potter can recreate the pot in a form that is new and undamaged.

God follows a similar approach in mending our broken lives. First he immerses us in the "water" of his Spirit. Then, when we are soft and pliable, he takes his gentle but strong hands and reduces the pot of our life back to a lump of clay, which he places on his potter's wheel. Only then can he spin us, work us, and firmly but gently begin molding us back into his beautiful image. The result is a beautiful work of art that will neither crack nor break. But to get to this point, we must let God take who we think we are, totally do away with that, and transform us.

Originally, it was God who created us, beautiful and whole. But these cracks have developed in our lives. The question we face now is whether we will allow God to reform our lives. Will we permit him to strip away our outward forms and delusions? Will we be vulnerable to his touch as he returns us to a seemingly formless lump of clay? Will we be patient while he reworks and molds us into the form he originally planned for us?

It takes great faith and trust to let your illusory self be dismantled while God recreates within you the beauty and innocence he desires for you. But if you will let go and let God, then using hands that are firm and gentle, he will lay them upon your wounded mass, your lump of formlessness and nothingness, and begin to reshape you into a beautiful work of art that is also functional and strong. Thus remade by God, your life will gradually cease to be marred by brokenness and will begin to be filled with love, joy, peace, goodness, beauty, and truth.

Will you allow yourself to be open to this reform? Let the child within you be awakened and reborn. Encourage this desire and hunger for spiritual renewal and growth to blossom within you.

If we open ourselves to him, he will fulfill all that is good and beautiful and true in us. We will be enlightened. We will be awakened. We will be born again.

# The Music of Creation

"IN THE BEGINNING, GOD CREATED . . ."

These five simple words are the opening of the most profound story of all: the history of the creation of the cosmos and of all humankind. The story originates in the Middle East but is honored around the world by disciples of Judaism, Christianity, and Islam.

Mystics in these three major monotheistic traditions believe that God's first act in creating the cosmos was producing harmonious sound. Faiths portray this music of creation in a variety of ways. Some call it the "music of the spheres." Hindu tradition describes Vishnu, one of the many Hindu deities, as holding a biwa (or stringed instrument), and creating the worlds through music.

The opening line of the Gospel of Saint John, the most mystical of the four New Testament gospels, hints at this concept when it describes the "Logos," an ancient term for "wisdom" often translated into English as "word":

> *In the beginning was the Word, and the Word was with God,*
> *and the Word was God.*

Nearly every one of the world's spiritual traditions teaches that there is an intimate connection between God's act of creating the cosmos and human creativity. There's a harmonic link between the music that we enjoy singing, listening to, or composing and the music of creation.

If music is a symphony of vibrations working in perfect harmony, proportion, and rhythm, then our earthly music is a mirror reflection of the original music of God. When it is working properly, our music comes from God's music and points back to God. But the Creator's music is beyond all description and all comparison. It is enveloping and inclusive. It is beyond awe. It is wonder and love. Its melody and harmony are in and through all creation for those who have the ears to hear.

One doesn't have to be a musician or a theologian to see that the idea of living in harmony with creation—and with creation's Creator—is one that can help us all live a more complete and spiritually grounded life.

## A PULSATING PLANET

CENTURIES AGO, science was largely concerned with describing the interaction of solids. Today, scientists and pioneers on the cutting edge of the "new physics" are increasing our ability to peer into the inner workings of much of the cosmos, and what they're finding there is a world of vibrations.

Music itself is a series of vibrations working in perfect harmony, proportion, and rhythm. Everything we hear consists of sound waves, and there is much that we can't even hear: subsonic waves move too slowly for us to perceive them, and supersonic sound waves move too rapidly.

The story of creation doesn't end with music. It continues when God says, "Let there be light." Less than three centuries ago, Isaac Newton "proved" that light consisted of particles. Now we know that light, like sound, is a series of vibrations and waves. These waves also move in different harmony, proportion, and rhythm to give us color. In a sense, even color and light are forms of music that are simply perceived by a different sense organ, the eye.

Science shows us that different creatures "see" and "hear" sights and sounds that are beyond human perception. Some of these creatures don't even use eyes to see or ears to hear. They utilize different organs to sense the vibrations and waves that are pulsing throughout all creation. "Pit" vipers sense the world through the pits around their nose and mouth. And certain bees are among the insects who sense light waves around different-colored flowers to lead them to the sweetest nectar. Such snapshots from nature confirm the mystics' belief that all is vibration, that all is harmony.

A musician I know once told me her own compositions have been influenced by her powerful visions and revelations. She told me how she had seen a vision of heaven, and when I asked her what it was like, she said she could see sound and hear color. She said trees and flowers made beautiful music, and when this music was created, it produced vibrant colors. In her vision, sound and sight had become one without losing the unique characteristics of either. Rather, what she experienced was a heightened reality that resembled but also expanded upon what we know in the here-and-now.

Visions like these reveal the deeper reality that everything in creation springs from the all-encompassing and ever-present music of God. Some of this may sound absurdly esoteric, but it's not. In fact, understanding creation is an essential part of understanding our own place and role in the cosmos.

After God composed the music of creation and illumined the cosmos with light, next came form. As the story of creation tells us, God created the earth, the waters, the sky, and the stars. Then came life in the waters and on the earth, including human life, which pulses with its own vital energy. In the beginning all was God's music, for it all came forth from the perfect harmony of love, existed within that love, and drew all back to love.

Once we have a true understanding of the mystical beauty and harmony of creation, we can learn how to break through from our often fragmentary experiences of life, and our often foggy notions of existence, to a much more holistic and integrated understanding of the harmony, balance, and proportion of all that God has made.

Once we see all these things more clearly, we can have a greater sense of our own divine purpose in the world. Instead of seeing the world as a jumble, or as a random convergence of chaos, we can begin to experience its wonderful beauty.

This sense of the beauty of creation isn't always evident in our daily lives. But it is something we all long for, and for good reason: We were created to experience and enjoy this harmony. A proper understanding of the Creator's work will provide us with the insight we need to find our way back to that mystical music of creation.

## CONNECTING WITH CREATION

As I WRITE these words, I'm sitting at a wooden desk and looking out the window of my monastic hermitage, which allows me to watch a hungry squirrel feasting on some kernels of hardened corn and observe the frenzied flight of a few birds. I'm separated from the scene by a pane of glass, but I feel powerfully connected to all the sights and colors that my eyes take in.

I'm not having what psychologists would call a "peak experience," which happens when someone has a powerful emotional reaction to the beauty of a piece of music, or the fragrance of a flower. I'm not even experiencing an epiphany, a term Irish-born James Joyce coined for those rare moments of revelation that allow us to see the essential inner nature of a person or thing. Rather, I'm going through something that is a deep, intuitive sense of the reality of the interconnectedness of everything I see, myself, and God.

For me, it's a mystical perspective that permeates everything I do. But I didn't always see things that way. Rather, it is something that evolved gradually over many years, beginning long before I knew what it all meant.

I remember when I was a six-year-old boy growing up in Oklahoma City. There was a concrete driveway that led to my parents' home, but there was a dirt-and-gravel area between the end of the driveway and the street. When it rained, this area would turn into a series of puddles that seemed like custom-designed receptacles for the pebbles I would throw in their direction. I can clearly recall one rainy day when I was hurling pebbles toward the puddles. Then, all of a sudden, everything just went *click*. Without any warning, the scene I was a part of connected deep inside of me. I didn't know what to make of it, but I experienced a connection to everything around me that I can still remember vividly to this very day.

Later, when I was ten years old, my parents were driving my older brother and sister to a camp in Indiana for the summer, and I went along for the ride. After we arrived at the camp, and while everyone else was taking care of logistics, I lay down on my side next to the camp's lake, looking over the surface of the water. Without any warning, I was overcome by an intuitive sensation of my connection with everything around me. I couldn't articulate precisely what happened, but somehow I knew it involved God.

A similar thing happened to me three or four years ago when I was sitting and praying on a bench in front of our hermitage. Suddenly, everything began to resonate together. The best way I know how to explain what happened is that the earth and everything in it began to shimmer, even though I knew nothing was shimmering visibly. Rather, it was the music of God's creation making itself known to me mystically as I prayed.

God often meets us when we pray. I have found that an ancient technique called breath prayer helps connect us to all of creation through the Spirit of God. In breath prayer, as I inhale and exhale I ask God to visit me, cleanse me, strengthen me, and use me for his glory.

Many major world religions practice some form of breath prayer. I find it interesting, though, that the Judeo-Christian scriptural tradition identifies "spirit"—whether it is God's Spirit or our own spirit—with "wind" and "breath." As we breathe deeply and pray, we reconnect to God's Spirit, which created and animates all. In doing so, we bring ourselves back into harmony with God and all creation.

## DIVINE HARMONY

EVERYTHING GOD has created reveals the divine imprint. The nature of creation manifests the unique signature of the Creator God, just as Picasso's signature in the corner of a painting reveals the work's origin. The harmony evident in our universe is evidence of the divine impetus behind all that exists. The music of creation reveals the interconnectedness of everything that God has made. But beyond that, this cosmic harmony also reveals the unity and melody that exist within the divine nature.

"God is one," say the ancient scriptures revered by Jews,

Christians, and Muslims. But this doesn't mean that divinity is single, or solitary. Rather, God's oneness is the result of unity amidst diversity, communality among plurality. That's the meaning of an otherwise confusing Old Testament verse, Genesis 1:26, in which God says, "Let us make [humankind] in our image, after our likeness." Here, God's self-description isn't singular but plural. God is one, but is made up of multiple persons.

In theological terms, this is expressed in the Christian doctrine of the Trinity, the concept of one God in three persons. This centuries-old tradition is one of the most beautiful and most misunderstood Christian beliefs, and is both basic and revolutionary. The concept of the Trinity explains how the harmony of creation is merely a reflection of the divine harmony existing among the three persons of the Creator God.

Over the past twenty centuries, a deep and impressive body of theological tradition has developed about the three persons of the Trinity, which are not understood as completely autonomous, separate, or self-sufficient beings, but rather as three distinct personae, or "masks," of God. These three persons are:

- The Father, who is the "fountain fullness" from which the other persons eternally flow. The Father flows from nothing. He is totally self-sufficient, as an eternal fountain that never runs dry.
- The Son is eternally begotten by the Father. He is, as one of the classic Christian creeds proclaims, "God from God, light from light, true God from true God. Begotten, not made." This does not refer to Jesus' Incarnation through the Virgin Mary. Rather, this begottenness has gone on from eternity, is occurring right now, and will continue forever.
- The Spirit proceeds eternally from the Father, from the Father through the Son, and from the love union of the Father and the Son.

Clearly, the doctrine of the Trinity is one of the most baffling and puzzling concepts in all Christian theology. During the past twenty centuries, some of the world's best minds have attempted to grasp and explain it. Perhaps mystics alone can truly grasp its meaning in their hearts.

I am reminded of a story from the life of Saint Augustine (A.D. 354–430). Augustine often preached about the Trinity while he was bishop of Hippo, which is near present-day Algeria. One day, the saint was praying and meditating as he walked along the beaches of the Mediterranean in between sermons. As he walked, he looked up and saw a little boy on the beach in front of him. The boy was taking a bucket, filling it with water in the ocean, and carrying the water back to the beach, where he would empty it into a hole he had dug in the sand.

Bishop Augustine approached the youngster and asked, "What are you doing?"

The boy answered, "I am going to take that big ocean and put it in that little hole."

Augustine was touched by the boy's innocence. Smiling patiently, he said, "You can't do that. That big ocean is too big to fit in that little hole."

The boy looked up from his work and said, "Easier for me to put that big ocean into this little hole than for you to take the big Trinity and put it into your little mind, Bishop Augustine."

With that, the boy vanished into thin air, for as the saint now recognized, he was not a little boy after all, but was an angel sent by God to remind the great bishop of how small and limited a thing the human mind is when it attempts to grasp the things of God.

I don't claim to comprehend the Trinity. Its deepest meanings have divided Eastern (or Orthodox) believers from those in the West for centuries. Still, for Christians East and West, the Trinity is an essential concept that holds the key to our understanding not only of the harmony of creation but also the complex connections within our own minds and souls. The concept of the Trinity also helps us understand how we can grow to love other members of the human family more deeply.

## OVERFLOWING LOVE

THE DIVINE SIGNATURE can be seen in all of creation; the Creator's unique imprint can be seen in our own lives. If we look carefully within our own hearts and minds, we can see a diversity of elements and faculties. In some ways, this diversity is similar to that which exists among the persons of the Trinity. Some theologians have even described humans as trinities of body, soul, and spirit.

Even though we all have these diverse elements within us, each of us remains one person, one being. When we are balanced and healthy, all our diverse elements and faculties function in harmony, proportion, and rhythm with the others. Our whole being becomes a harmony mirroring the harmony of creation. Our life becomes a song.

Unfortunately, things within us can go out of tune. When inner harmony and balance are replaced by disunity and fragmentation, the result is chaos and cacophony. Instead of body, soul, and spirit working together as one, there is conflict and turmoil.

The Trinity, however, is a representation of the divine plan for how the distinct parts of our personality are supposed to work together in harmony, giving us a tangible image of God's intention for humanity.

The Trinity shows us that love is at the foundation of God, and of all that is. "God is love," writes Saint John in his first epistle, and as Saint Paul writes in Romans, "Love is the fulfillment of the law," a brief but surprisingly profound sentence. Elsewhere in John's

Gospel, Jesus tells us, "The greatest commandment is love." To miss this is to miss God.

God is the only being in our universe who is infinite, eternal, and totally self-sufficient. When we hear the term self-sufficient, many of us picture someone who is self-absorbed or self-enclosed. But that doesn't describe God. God is supremely good. And it is God's bountiful goodness that causes his love to diffuse and emanate outward throughout all of creation.

God loves as God creates: freely, joyously, spontaneously, and beautifully. God didn't have to create the cosmos, and God doesn't have to love the cosmos or those who inhabit it. Rather, the Father's love flows to the Son and the Spirit, patterning the ways in which the Creator's harmony infuses all of creation. In the same way, our love should freely flow outward, touching everyone we meet, and mirroring the love of God expressed within the life of the Trinity.

We see this kind of divine love lived out in human experience in the family, the most basic of all human communities and an important institution often called "the domestic church" by the Church itself. Marriage, which is honored by the Church as a great sign—or mystical sacrament—of God's love for humanity, is designed to be a powerful relationship in which man and woman seek each other's best interests by practicing self-emptying. As husband and wife die to self, and as they sacrifice for each other, new life is created for both, and a third is produced. Two mutually *die to self* for the other, from which at least a third proceeds. When couples are blessed with children, these offspring wonderfully symbolize the creative power of self-emptying, self-diffusive love.

God's goodness requires at least one other for his love to be self-diffusive, or not self-centered. God's love requires that two join in selfless union to produce at least a third. Transcendence requires that this all be fulfilled within the self-sufficiency of the One God.

Thus, the Trinity is a perfect fulfillment of God's goodness, love, and transcendence in a way that still keeps his oneness intact.

Another place where human love is exhibited is within Christian community. The Church forms an umbrella over everything in our lives. It is not something we join, or a club we belong to, it is our very life. There are many expressions of community within the Church, such as associations of the faithful, and various renewal groups and movements. Next to the family, it is the community of faith that can most powerfully express God's love.

It is in the mystery—and often the messiness—of these human relationships that God's transcendence, goodness, and love become tangible, bringing us into deeper connection with God, with humanity, and with creation. Ideally, our human relationships will reflect the music of creation just as the Trinity reflects the perfect balance, harmony, proportion, and rhythm that exist among three divine persons.

The music human musicians compose is created for the ears, the emotions, the mind, and the soul. But the music of creation must sink into the deepest realms of our spirit, where it is better understood by intuition than by emotion or thought. Here, working deep within us, this music of creation will bring us into harmony with all of creation, with our human brothers and sisters, and with the Creator God.

# The Harmony
# of Human Life

ALL CREATION EXHIBITS THE HARMONY AND BALANCE OF God. This divine music overflows into the cosmos, reflecting God's traces in everything that is.

You and I participate in this cosmic harmony of God in a very special manner. God created us, and each of us reflects the traces of the divine image in a unique way. The opening chapter of Genesis reveals to us the Creator's thoughts about the creation of humanity when it says, "Let us make [humankind] in our image, after our likeness."

What is this passage trying to tell us? What does it mean to be created in God's image? What *is* God's image, anyway? For millennia, poets, artists, philosophers, and theologians have wrestled with these questions.

Some have said it is our capacity for rational thought that makes us stand out from the rest of creation. Others have said it is humans' impressive capacity to communicate through language that makes us unique in creation. Still others have said it is our power to love that makes us unique. But many animals exhibit commonsense behavior, sophisticated communication, and what seems to be self-sacrificial love. And humans often fail to be rational, communicative, and loving. None of these explanations—or even all three together—tells the whole story of humanity's unparalleled state among all of creation.

I believe that what makes humanity unique is that it bears the image of God in an amazing way. As a Christian who is a devoted student of the Judeo-Christian scriptures and traditions, one way for me to describe that uniqueness is by considering the parallel that exists between the triune God and our own triune nature. When the Trinitarian God said, "Let us make [humankind] in our image," we were created with three primary faculties: body, soul, and spirit.

This threefold division is implied but not absolute. The Fathers of the Church often speak only of body and soul but divide the soul into a lower and higher faculty corresponding to soul and spirit. They also emphasize that the human being constitutes an organic and spiritual unity that cannot be artificially divided into mutually exclusive compartments.

Regardless of whether we think human nature is twofold or threefold, understanding how our distinct faculties were designed by our Creator can help us learn how to live a harmonious, God-centered life. When we do this, our own lives will embody the cosmic harmony that is so evident in all of creation.

In our lives, there are many times when we see the close connections between our various faculties. I have seen that when my mind is overflowing with beautiful thoughts, my emotions often follow along and I experience joy and peace. But when I am troubled by agitated thoughts, my emotions can become disturbed.

When I am troubled, I have found that taking a few deep breaths, calling on the power of the Holy Spirit, and releasing my thoughts and emotions to him is a way to calm down both my raging emotions and the powerful adrenaline rushes that sometimes upset my body. Thus our various faculties are interconnected. You can't separate body, soul, and spirit with a surgical knife, just as we cannot separate the three persons of the one triune God.

We can achieve the harmony God desires for us by understanding ourselves better, and to do that, it helps to understand each of the three human faculties:

The *body* is the physical part of our being. It is where we live, and it is the location of our action. In addition to our physicality, the body incorporates elements people don't always think of as physical, such as our emotions and passions, which science convincingly shows us are largely chemical. There is even a physical aspect to thought, which is produced in the brain with the help of electricity and chemicals.

According to Christian tradition, the body, in its present form, is impermanent. "All flesh is like grass," said Jesus. Yet someday in the future, our bodies will be resurrected and renewed, much as Jesus' body was transformed after his resurrection. The Gospel passages that describe Christ's post-Resurrection body aren't as detailed as we might like, but they clearly portray a body that is recognizable by people who knew Jesus yet is somehow different. Christians throughout the ages, particularly those who have endured physical disabilities or suffering, have looked forward to this promised bodily resurrection.

The *soul* is the seat of cognition and thought. Thought is influenced by our physical body, but our cognitive awareness and our innate sensitivity to all that is around us in the world are based in the soul. You can even look at the soul as a halfway point between the body and the spirit, building on the physical aspects of life, but pointing us toward the spiritual dimensions of existence.

Through the centuries, the words "mind" and "soul" have been used interchangeably by philosophers, such as the Franciscan thinker Saint Bonaventure, whose book *Journey of the Soul to God* has also been called *Journey of the Mind to God*.

Teachers have told me, "The struggle for the soul begins in the mind." Frequently it is our thoughts that play an influential role in the nature and tendencies of our souls. Thoughts are impermanent to a certain degree and often remain fixated on transient realities of space and time. For now, our minds shuffle between the passing and the eternal, the finite and the infinite, the body and the spirit, but in heaven our minds will transcend the limits of space and time, existing in the infinite and eternal.

The *spirit* is the inner essence of the human being. It is deeper than thought, emotion, or action and is also beyond them Spirit is the place of pure intuition, beyond thought, emotion or action, beyond concept, word, and form. It is the most genuine self. It is the real "me" in me, and the real "you" in you. It is being itself. It is that which makes us most a person without being limited to personality.

I continually witness the connections between my own body, soul, and spirit. I am both a musician and a singer. I am also a teacher. Fulfilling these responsibilities utilizes all aspects of my being. But suppose I were to lose my hands, so that I could not play the guitar. Would this make me less "me"? Or suppose I lost my voice, so I could neither sing nor teach. Would this make me lose my uniqueness in God's sight? Or suppose I injured a part of my brain, so that my emotions became confused, or I could no longer grasp or teach all the things I currently talk about. Would I lose the essence of myself? Would I no longer be me? Would I no longer have genuine value or worth?

My music is truly me. It communicates something that is central to my being. My teaching is truly me as well, and through teaching I communicate concepts and visions that are a very important part of who I am. My emotions are also me, and they reflect my own values about life and God. All of these various aspects reflect me, and to some degree, even are me. They are part of what the Eastern Christian mystics call my energies. But they are not the essence of me.

If I were to lose any or all of these energies or abilities, my essence would remain. I would still be me. The core of my being would remain always. The same is true for you.

## BETWEEN TIME AND ETERNITY

THIS INNER ESSENCE of our spirit is beyond space and time. Our spirits already exist in eternity and infinity, even though our bodies and minds still exist here on earth in space and time. Our spirit is beyond concepts, ideas, words, and emotions. It transcends all these things, but it directs and animates them all, particularly when we are seeking to live in accordance with God's plan for creation and the image in which we were created.

So many of us live our lives in an environment of noise, disorder, and chaos. But we can only find the human harmony God intended for us through silence and stillness. Paradoxically, it is stillness that orders our actions; solitude that creates true human community as God's family; unknowing that makes our knowledge pure and holy.

Through silence, solitude, and stillness, we may discover the divine harmony God intended for us and allow it to direct our thoughts, words, and deeds. Buddhists call this nirvana, a state they describe as a nonbeing that is fully alive, a nondoing that is fully active. This type of inner stillness and solitude was an important part of how God originally intended life to be, and it brings us peace, fulfillment, and joy. But our bodies, souls, and spirits have been corroded by the effects of sin and evil, and our lives confused by the confusion and cacophony of modern life.

Eastern Christian mystical theology says that the spirit is, by nature, fitted for infinity and eternity. We are, these mystics say, by nature pure and God-directed. Still, sin and evil are real. Our bodies and souls are easily sullied and need to be cleansed through spiritual disciplines.

During the course of living life, the spirit gets locked up within the body and soul. It gets covered up and suffocated beneath the commotion and debris of life. And many people go through life almost totally unaware of the spirit's existence. But it never dies, and except in the case of demonic possession, it remains pure and clean. When the body and soul are redirected through spiritual discipline, the spirit is set free, allowing it to breathe and to exist in the infinite and eternal again.

I love the words of Jesus that say we must become a child to enter the kingdom of God. We must be born again. Spiritual rebirth is enlightenment, which changes our whole perception of life, reintegrating the human trinity of body, soul, and spirit. Life is reordered, so that the spirit—not the body—becomes the animating principle. Only then can our true spiritual nature—the inner child of God—be the source and directing principle of all we do, with the body and soul becoming actualizing agents performing the way and will of God.

As we'll see in more detail later, all of this happens through the work of Jesus the Son and the gift of the Holy Spirit, which lead us back into full communion and integration with and in the Father, our Creator. God's Spirit awakens our spirit. Jesus the Son shows body and soul what to do, how to think and feel. And the Father shows the newly reborn and reintegrated human self the source of all life, his own fountain fullness.

## REDISCOVERING THE LOST
## INNER CHILD OF GOD

JESUS SAID that we must become children to enter the kingdom of heaven. For each of us, our spirit represents the inner child of God. But many of us spend much of our lives out of touch with this inner child. Some of us even become oblivious to its existence. We forget it is there at all. Our life becomes a clutter of jumbled and unimportant ideas and activities. Thoughts, emotions, and actions go wild and begin to choke the very life out of us, and those around us.

But Jesus opens the way for us to be enlivened and enlightened, to be born again. Through spiritual rebirth our spirit—the inner child—is rediscovered and given its proper place in the human trinity of body, soul, and spirit. Then and only then do we begin to make the real music of God within our very being.

Interestingly, many Catholic Christian scholars have told me that they believe this threefold understanding of human nature creates a unique opportunity for dialogue with the millions of disciples of Eastern religions. The Christian belief in a spirit or essence that is beyond our comprehension opens up the door to talk with those whose theology differs with ours on many points. For example, Christians believe that both body and spirit are eternal. Most Eastern faiths, however, believe that only the spirit is eternal, and the body is temporary and transient. Still, disciples of both traditions affirm that spirit should have supremacy over body, and that human life achieves fullness and integration when the body and soul orbit around the nucleus of the spirit.

Certainly, only God can teach us the balance and harmony of the life-giving music that he intended for us to experience. By the rebirth and ongoing renewal of our spirit, we can know the same kind of divine harmony that the cosmos enjoys. Soon we can bring God's rhythm and proportion to all we are, encounter, or touch. Thus the music of God spreads from one person, circumstance, and situation to another, until it reaches every corner of the cosmos. As Saint Paul wrote, "Creation awaits with eager expectation the revelation of the children of God."

Jesus becomes the way, the truth, and the life to reconcile all of creation with the fullness of the Godhead. Just as the Trinity, one God in three persons, created the cosmos, so this triune God created us with our triune nature.

God designed our bodies, souls, and spirits to work in perfect balance, rhythm, and proportion, with our spirits being primary, our souls being secondary, and our bodies serving spirit and soul. Thus, life was designed to be a symphony in which each of us has a part, creating one divine music with many eternal harmonies.

This is bliss and joy. This is paradise. This is the music of life for which God created us.

# Life Out of Balance

ONE WOULD THINK THAT EVERYONE WOULD WANT TO JOIN in with God to enjoy the universal harmony of creation, working together with God to produce the beautiful music of the cosmos.

Anyone who has ever taken music lessons knows that no one can force you to play real music. A demanding teacher can make you practice scales or coerce you to perform a particular composition. But for music to be truly beautiful, it must be made freely, out of goodness and love, not fear or compulsion.

Very early in our history, humanity chose to stop making the divine music that had come so naturally to us from the very beginning of time. We decided we wanted to make our own music in our own way. Far from improving on the melodies of the Master Musician, our decision produced discord instead of harmony, imbalance rather than rhythm, deformity instead of the beauty and proportion the Creator intended for us to enjoy.

In the Bible, this problem is symbolized by such events as the disobedience of Adam and Eve and their expulsion from the Garden of Eden—events theologians describe as the Fall. Human disharmony is further symbolized by Biblical accounts of the murder of Abel by his brother Cain. From these beginnings, a whole series of negative, self-centered, and outright destructive events begin to take place in human history. These rebellions have affected all of humankind and indeed every aspect of creation ever since.

Specifically, the body—not the spirit—became our primary motivator, as passions and lusts began to creep into and control our thoughts, emotions, and desires. Our soul became secondary, following where the body led as thoughts became confused, disordered, and focused solely on the self instead of higher things. The spirit—that pure, original inner child of God—got covered over and forgotten, unable to be free or breathe the clear air of the Holy Spirit.

This is what we call original sin. In the end, it brought death instead of life, sickness rather than health, dysfunction rather than the harmonious, creative beauty of God's all-encompassing music.

Not all religions or spiritual traditions use the terms "Fall" and "original sin," but just about all of them agree that something has gone horribly wrong with our lives and our world. Call it what you will, the result is the same. The reality is self-evident. Our world needs to be fixed and set straight. Our lives need to be transformed, to be brought back into some kind of divine harmony and order once again.

Most thinkers throughout human history have agreed that this pervasive, powerful problem is the main reason humanity has religion in the first place. Although the world's faiths don't always agree, they are absolutely unanimous in their belief that humanity needs help and instruction from someone who can show us how to begin making God's music again.

Only when we are spiritually transformed and renewed can our lives be brought into harmony and balance again. And from our harmonious lives, our divine music can spread to others, including those among all peoples and lands, throughout all time and space.

In a sense, our earthly lives are an extended practice session, a spiritual rehearsal for eternity, where we will make this infinite music in an infinite way within infinity itself.

## A UNIVERSAL PROBLEM; DIFFERENT BUT SIMILAR SOLUTIONS

NEARLY ALL of the world's faith traditions deal with the problems Christianity calls the Fall and original sin. Although they come at these problems in different ways, there is surprising agreement on the fact that humanity is in trouble and needs divine help.

*Taoism* tells us of a mythical land that existed in the beginning of time. In that pure and pristine place, everyone was naturally in a state of perfect harmony and balance, without contrivance or effort. But this pristine state of affairs was short-lived. Part of the problem, according to Taoism, was that we began labeling everything as either good or bad. Then, as we acted on this rigid duality, the bad drew us farther away from the good. At the same time, that which was good often became puffed up and self-righteous, and as a result, goodness became contrived rather than innocent, so it was no longer truly good. Soon everything was so out of balance that the confusion enveloped not only all of humanity but all of creation as well.

In its centuries-old descriptions of the problems in the natural world, Taoism contains some eerily relevant portrayals of the ecological and environmental crises that, in modern times, have been exacerbated by consumerism and industry. The result is that everything reaches a point of crisis, a breaking point where neither people nor the planet can take much more.

The way back to paradise, Taoism teaches, is through learning the discipline of nonaction, "non-ado" or non-contrivance in meditation, movement, ritual, and lifestyle. Through the quiet, internal discipline of non-ado, there is a gradual return to the original balance of Heaven and Earth, yang and yin, the positive and the negative.

*Buddhism*, too, has a rather negative view of our current state of affairs. Like Hinduism, a faith with which it has deep connections, Buddhism teaches that there are hundreds of thousands of distinct eras and worlds called kalpas. Our present world is only one of these, but it is believed to be the darkest, most unenlightened, and oppressive world in all of cosmic history. The only places darker than ours are the domains of demons, or "the hells," which are dark and destructive realms that make Dante's *Inferno* look pleasant by comparison.

Our problem is that we have been almost completely blinded by our own unchecked desire. As a result, we are caught in a constant existence of sufferings.

Buddhism has a belief in reincarnation, a perpetual process of death and rebirth. Those who are alive as people now face the possibility of coming back to earth in a future life as an animal or an insect. But being born a human being is believed to be extraordinarily good news, and the "Buddha," or the "enlightened" one, shows us a way out of our desire and the consequences of our suffering. It is up to us to respond and make amends.

*Judaism*, along with the Christian tradition, speaks of humanity's banishment from paradise in powerful and poetic terms. According to the book of Genesis, the Fall—human history's most tragic event—is told through the story of Adam and Eve in the Garden of Eden.

The garden is "good." It is a paradise created by God. The serpent in the story symbolizes Satan and other demonic spirits who were once great angels but fell from grace themselves through their unquenchable desire to have things their way and their rebellion against God. The serpent tempts Adam and Eve—God's final and greatest creation—to follow in Satan's footsteps rather than God's. How was such a defection accomplished?

## PARADISE LOST

ACCORDING TO GENESIS, the serpent tempted Adam and Eve to eat of a tree in the Garden of Eden that God had told them not to eat from. Throughout the ages, novels, plays, and movies have portrayed the fall as a sexual temptation, but this is literary license. The real sin in the Garden of Eden was humanity's insistence on usurping the place of God. "The moment you eat of it," the serpent promised, "your eyes will be opened and you will be like gods who know what is good and what is bad" (GENESIS 3:5).

Only God can truly know good or evil absolutely by his own power, for only God is all-knowing. With their own wisdom, apart from God, Adam and Eve claimed to be all-knowing, or "like God." This is the ultimate arrogance and pride. It was human pride, not sexual temptation, that was the true original sin.

God knows immediately what Adam and Eve have done, and he confronts them. He forgives them and shows them mercy but does not protect them from the natural consequences of their sin. Humanity has set itself on a course that must now be played out. There is no turning back.

As a result of their choice, the first humans were ushered out of the garden and barred from returning. An angelic being with flaming, revolving swords guards the gate of heaven and protects the "tree of life," which held the secret to eternal life. For the rest of her life, Eve will experience pain in childbirth, symbolizing bodily sickness. Whereas once working in the Garden of Eden was joyful and effortless, Adam will now see that work was something done "by the sweat of your face." Passions, or "urges," were now out of rational or spiritual control. These undisciplined desires imprisoned the spirit. Finally, physical death—which had been previously unknown—came into the world. Now, not only Adam and Eve but all who would come after them would experience both bodily and spiritual death.

Christian tradition teaches that through the Fall, humanity lost its preternatural gifts. Once, it had been our *natural* response to simply do God's will in all things. Doing the right thing was simply our spontaneous, normal response to life. Goodness didn't require discipline or exertion. Can you imagine not being tempted to eat that second (or third) helping of dessert? Or not immediately reacting in anger when someone cuts you off on the highway or jumps in front of you in the line at the grocery store? Or innately desiring the best for everyone, not just for yourself? Before the Fall, our natural and immediate response was to simply "be," and to do the right thing.

Now we still have the desire to do the right thing, for we are created in God's image and inwardly seek the things of God. But that godly desire is trapped and imprisoned with a wall of disordered flesh, emotions, and destructive thought processes. The spirit is no longer our primary driving force. It is covered over or forgotten.

Our bodies and souls are also changed by the Fall. The soul is disjointed and confused within itself. The body loses its original God-given beauty and innocence, a loss we try to cover over with often futile efforts to cosmetically enhance our appearance. In short, Adam and Eve's banishment from the paradise of the Garden of Eden isn't a long-ago fairy tale. It's an existential, cosmic reality, and it's something we experience in the here and now of everyday life.

## DIMMED, OR DAMNED?

THROUGH THE CENTURIES, Christian thinkers have used two distinct types of analogies or parables to describe the effects of sin and grace in the human soul.

One analogy was used by Saint Bonaventure, a Franciscan mystic who lived during the thirteenth and fourteenth centuries. Bonaventure saw the human soul as a mirror originally created to reflect, in a very special way, the image of God. And he saw sin as the dust and dirt that can dim the clarity of the mirror's reflection, and possibly even obscure the reflection of God's image completely.

It's a simple but meaningful analogy, and it's very hopeful. While acknowledging that sin can cut us off from spiritual truth, it doesn't portray God as a vengeful deity who destroys our mirrors at the first sign of disobedience.

The good news is that Jesus cleanses our mirror so that we can clearly reflect God's image once again. And no matter how thick the dirt may pile up on the mirror, way down deep the human soul always maintains the God-given capacity to reflect the divine image again. All that's required is that we be cleansed, a transformation that comes through the forgiveness of sins offered by Jesus.

A second and quite different analogy from the mirror analogy described above comes from the early Lutherans in Germany and the early Swiss Calvinists. These sincere (and often severe) men of God were trying to illustrate the devastating effects of sin on the human soul, and our desperate need for God's forgiving grace. Unfortunately, they unintentionally created a picture of condemnation and judgment that leads many to despair and despondency rather than repentance and renewal.

These religious leaders described the sinful human soul as a pile of dung. The gracious forgiveness of Christ was pictured as a thin layer of snow covering the human dung pile. And thanks to this sprinkling of snow, when God the Father looks down at us from the heights of heaven, he sees not the dung that makes up the pile, but the thin snow covering, and looks upon us as if we were a pile of pure white snow.

The many theological and psychological problems with this analogy are quite unfortunate. First, it portrays Christ's grace (the snow) as superficial at best. Second, it reduces the human soul to a pile of dung. Even after being reborn in Jesus, we remain essentially a pile of rotting waste. As opposed to the mirror analogy, we're not dirt-smudged reflectors who await God's cleansing so we can gloriously shine with the beauty of God. Rather, we are thoroughly corrupted and unclean.

This understanding of human nature and sin has created vast psychological ramifications in America, a country that was founded largely on the Protestant world view. The dung analogy has either knowingly or unknowingly been used by many of the churches that were part of our early history. It even found its way into Catholic theology through Jansenism, a heresy proclaiming that human nature is totally depraved.

As a result, many of us were trained to think poorly about ourselves and others. But deep inside, some could see that this approach somehow wasn't quite right. And after time, like a spring

that had been held down before breaking free, there was a powerful reaction (or even overreaction) in the opposite direction.
Instead of wallowing in self-degradation, some embraced untram-
meled egoism, which is almost always a psychological mask to cover
a low self-image. Instead of seeing ourselves as dung, some of us
began seeing ourselves as gods.

Today, the unfortunate ramifications of the dung analogy have
spawned a whole post-Reformation culture that is torn apart inside
in two opposite and equally unhealthy directions. On the one hand
is a destructively low self-image, and on the other an unrealistic and
unchecked egoism. Either way, these are formulas for personal and
spiritual disaster.

## THE SECRET OF SIN

SIN IS REAL. Those who try to pretend it doesn't exist are fool-
ing themselves. But to overstate its effects on the soul also does a
great disservice to the soul—and to God, who created us and loves
us enough to redeem us. Sin is not greater than God or God's
love.

The proper response to original sin, to the Fall, and to humanity's expulsion from paradise isn't an all-encompassing egoism or an
all-defeating self-loathing but rather a return to a more ancient,
holistic, and time-tested solution based on faith in the grace of
Christ and in the ministry of the Church.

Perhaps we need a fresh understanding of the whole notion of
sin. "Sin" was originally a word used during archery tournaments to
indicate that an archer's arrow had missed the desired target. Most
of the time, the arrow had gone in the right general direction, and
it may even have hit one of the outer circles on the target. But sin,
in archery terms, meant that the archer had missed the bull's-eye.

It's the same with us. Because we are created in God's image, we seek the things of God: goodness, truth, beauty, justice, mercy, and love. "All have sinned and are deprived of the glory of God," wrote Saint Paul (ROMANS 3:23). We have fallen short of the bull's eye of total centeredness and perfection.

This is a far cry from the dung analogy, or the language of some contemporary TV preachers, who loudly proclaim that all of us are hell-bent reprobates who have allowed sin to take us 180 degrees away from God and propel us in the opposite direction at supersonic speeds.

Actually, very few people turn totally away from God in favor of unmitigated evil and darkness. It does happen, but in my experience it is the exception and not the rule. Most of us are trying to do a good thing, but we miss, and we end up with less than perfect results. And often our missing winds up hurting those we love.

Rather than viewing human sinfulness as total depravity or absolute commitment to running away from God to embrace evil, I prefer to see the human predicament as a tire that is not balanced or properly centered. At first, a slightly off-balance tire is hardly noticeable. But if left uncorrected, it will make driving difficult, and then dangerous. That danger can lead to injury and even death.

Sin is the same. It can begin as a small imbalance or defect, but if left unchecked, it can make life difficult, and ultimately deadly.

Sin is real, but its seriousness should neither be overemphasized nor underemphasized. These extremes lead to real problems: one leads to self-loathing, the other to self-deification. Both prevent us from finding real relief and renewal in God.

## A CURSE ON ALL CREATION

It wasn't only Adam and Eve who fell at the Fall. Original sin has hurt everyone and everything.

In human society, the effects of sin are obvious. Not only is there great beauty, nobility, and compassion in humanity; there is also great selfishness, arrogance, brutality, and violence. Violence rages from the "civilized" cities of the so-called First World to the isolated bush villages of the Third World. It is present in the way men abuse and mistreat women, their parents, and their children. And human sinfulness is readily present in the pointless and de-structive wars that rage between tribes, regions, races, and nations.

There's no earthly utopia that gives a reprieve from the effects of the Fall.

I live in a remote monastic community in the wooded forests of the Ozark Mountains. Part of our income comes from farming, which may make some people think we've got a bucolic paradise here. But even a brief look around our corner of creation illustrates the far-reaching effects of the Fall.

The briefest glimpse through the window of my hermitage may reveal birds, insects, rabbits, or squirrels in the unrelenting and often violent drama of staying alive. "Eat or be eaten" is the rule of the jungle. I'll never forget the time I saw a sweat-drenched deer streak past my window, running for his life in frantic fear, trying des-perately to elude pursuing dogs used by us, the human hunter.

As many Christian thinkers through the ages have said, we live with the constant tension between the beauty of God's original creation and the horrible consequences of the Fall. The yin and the yang, the negative and the positive, death and life, the dark and the light, all are parts of the ongoing drama of cosmic evolution.

I don't believe that our current situation is the way creation was meant to be. Such a world doesn't match seeds of God's beauty and truth, seeds planted deep within our very souls that teach us to long for a world that's far more gentle, loving, and peaceful. Still, I can join my voice with the Psalmist, who wrote the following in one of his many prayers of thanksgiving to God: "I praise you. So wonderfully you made me; wonderful are your works!"

# Our Quest for God

THE STORY OF HUMANITY HAS BEEN OUR NEVER-ENDING, epic struggle to make the journey back to harmony with God. For each of us, this journey is a personal and individual pilgrimage. It is also unique: no two journeys are exactly the same. At the same time, the desire to return to God is one of the few true universals of human history.

We all seek to leave the sadness and sorrow of spiritual emptiness and seek the clear, fresh air of heaven. Although we might express it in different ways, we all long for the recovery of our lost innocence and the rebirth of the inner child of God. And we inherently seek the things of God—beauty and truth, justice and mercy, simplicity and innocence, goodness and love—because we were created to do so.

There are always scoffers deriding those who are driven by

strong spiritual desires. To their minds, such things seem irrational, unreal, or out of touch with the law of the jungle and the "real" world of brutality, self-centeredness, and aggression.

For most people, though, something deep within inspires them to look beyond the superficial, impermanent, and often illusory phenomena of time and matter to the eternal and infinite mystery of the Creator of all that is.

It is this quest for the divine that is the genesis of humanity's religious impulse. This quest first appears in ancient, prehistoric forms of spirituality such as shamanism, paganism, and animism. In a slightly different form, this quest also inspired philosophy, as thinkers through the centuries have sought to understand and explain the nature of reality and our role in the cosmos. Next came polytheism, with its belief in many gods. And thousands of years ago, the Jews introduced the concept of pure monotheism, a bequest that writer Thomas Cahill, author of *The Gifts of the Jews*, calls "the cornerstone of Western civilization," though other religions also spoke of one God at times.

Archaeology demonstrates the universality of this religious impulse. With the advent of the city and "civilization," as we call it, human life was organized around sacred sites, ritual landscapes, or the temples of the gods and goddesses. From the stone megaliths of Stonehenge on the gently rolling hills of southern England, to the majestic Mayan temples of the forests of Central America, to Europe's great medieval cathedrals, secular life was always centered on life of the spirit—at least until very recent times, when shopping malls and corporate skyscrapers have come to dominate the human environment.

Still, the quest continues. "My heart is restless until it rests in you," wrote Saint Augustine, a man who experimented with the sensuality of materialism and the consolations of philosophy before coming to faith in God.

In the Judeo-Christian tradition, there's a term we use to describe this pervasive spiritual impulse, and that term is "natural religion." Just as it's natural for a hungry person to eat, or for a sick person to seek out the help of a healer or doctor, it's the natural tendency of humanity to reach up to God.

This reaching out to God is itself inspired by the working of God in and around our lives and by the divine spark placed within us by our Creator. This is the spark that has ignited the many different religious traditions and faiths.

## IN THE BEGINNING

THE MAJESTY and mysteries of creation led the earliest humans to wonder about God. All creation points to the Creator, and from the earliest days, the desire for beauty, goodness, truth, and justice has led us to seek out a higher source from which these things flow. Ancient religions and philosophies all reveal something of the nature of God.

Most important, primitive religion teaches us of the existence of the spirit world and its connections with our world. The natural elements of fire, air, and water have long been held to possess spiritual counterparts, along with mountains, lakes, and fields, which people have long believed to be the abode of spirits. And as we learn from ancient tombs like Ireland's 5,000-year-old Newgrange, which was built before Egypt's pyramids, humans have long believed that death is not the end of life but just the beginning of another stage of existence. Something substantial about us survives to live again.

The ancient philosophers used their rational powers to make sense of the cosmos. To them, some concept of God simply made common sense. God was the constant that unified all the various aspects of the universe. He was the order that made sense of confusion and chaos. He was the all-encompassing First Principle, the source from which all individual principles came.

Each philosopher expressed these concepts in his own unique way. According to Aristotle, God could be found by following the particulars of creation back to the universal Creator. Plato, on the other hand, would proclaim that those same particulars of creation only begin to make sense when seen from the perspective of the universal First Principle. For Pythagoras, God was ultimate mathematical perfection, and the Therapeutes stressed contemplation of the divine, saying that truth must be found in an environment of apathia, or stillness, whether that stillness be communal or private.

Pope John Paul II recently reaffirmed that these philosophers' search for truth was indeed part of humanity's spontaneous religious impulse, and the questions they asked can be used by Christians today to help us ask the right questions about the challenges of human existence.

## FROM PHILOSOPHY TO RELIGION

THE WORLD'S MAJOR FAITHS are expressions of humanity's ongoing spiritual quest. Superficially, these faiths may seem opposed to one another, but they also share many similarities on a much deeper level—the level of humanity's universal and mystical longing for God.

The religious tradition Westerners refer to as *Hinduism* is an ancient and complex faith that contains many polytheistic and tritheistic elements, from which emerged both the monistic and the monotheistic. Hinduism speaks of the multidimensional nature of God that prefigures the Trinity and the need for unity amid diversity. Its message of both God's plurality and God's oneness is a powerful illustration of the truth that neither people nor gods need to be carbon copies of one another for them to love one another and work together.

Likewise, the tension between God's personal knowability on the one hand and God's impersonal unreachableness in human terms on the other speak to us of a God who is both relevant and transcendent.

Hinduism has much to say about the spiritual life as it teaches ways to approach God through the yoga of knowledge and study, through devotion and love, through meditation and contemplation, or through the justice of merciful action and service, to name but a few. In addition, the faith describes four successive stations of life—religious student, family person, householder, and holy man—showing that each period of one's life offers appropriate opportunities for religious devotion and action.

Our community operates a retreat center called More Mountain. We have found that many people attend one of our retreats as they find themselves at turning points in their lives. Some who come to More Mountain are newly married and are seeking ways to integrate spiritual disciplines into their family routines. Others are recently retired people who believe this new chapter of their lives offers them an exciting time to refocus on the things of Jesus in a more deliberate way. Often as I talk to these people about their lives, I find myself appreciating the way Hinduism describes the four stages of life.

*Buddhism* in its various forms is one of the fastest-growing faiths in the West, as seekers are attracted to its ancient heritage and often exotic rituals and traditions.

Buddhism points us toward a relationship with that which Christians might call God. It affirms a reality in God, humanity, and creation beyond the personal and the knowable, a reality that can only be "known" through intuitive meditation. The relationship between the individual and this unknowable reality can be deeply intimate and personal, but Buddhism places the ultimate responsibility for personal growth not on others—be they gods, spirits, or organizations—but squarely on the shoulders of each person. One of the greatest lessons Buddhism has to teach us is that the problem of human suffering is caused by our own unchecked desires. The solution it proposes is a program of moderate discipline, the Middle Way, that brings inner peace and liberation from our slavery to runaway desire. In many ways, Buddhism is more of a human discipline than an overt religion. This makes it an approach that can be practiced by nearly anyone—regardless of personal beliefs—which also helps propel its growing popularity in the West.

Taoism and Confucianism are the two great belief systems of China, which have had a profound impact on the whole of Asia and even the world. Taoism describes many mystical aspects of God and challenges humanity to make a personal response. Confucianism emphasizes strict ethical and social standards. Both faiths speak of the Tao, or the Way, which is personal in nature when it comes to the things of creation, and impersonal when it deals with issues like divine transcendence and eternity.

Taoism teaches that the world was originally a primordial paradise of goodness, but that people turned away from this goodness to practice cunning and self-centeredness. Next, spiritual leaders began devising definitions of good and evil, but things only got worse as people used sophistry to give lip service to these moral distinctions while their hearts went farther away from the true sources of goodness. The solution Taoist leaders proposed to correct this problem was an approach to life that stressed simplicity, quietness, and stillness. Our best action, they taught, was nonaction, non-contrivance, and stillness. Through such "non-ado," we gradually settle back into the original Way, or Tao, of the cosmos.

Things like meditation, yoga, martial arts, and herbal medicine help us cooperate with the Tao underlying all creation.

Confucianism weaves a system of ethical and social principles from the fabric of the Tao. First taught by Confucius during a time when China was enduring tremendous social chaos and barbaric tribal wars, Confucianism was a back-to-basics movement that looked longingly to a "golden age" of China's past, from which it drew its hope for the future.

This tradition teaches the way of intentional and deliberate goodness through the practice of justice, truth, compassion, and other virtues. In addition, there is a special emphasis on appropriate humility and the restoration of the relationships that give society its order. Confucianism teaches that more can be accomplished by subservience than rebellion. Thus, wives should serve their husbands, children their parents, youth their elders, and citizens their rulers. By changing these relationships through humility and service rather than by force, military strength, or rebellion, civilization could be restored.

This is particularly striking in light of the fact that Confucianism was born at a time when China endured incredible upheaval. Ironically, Confucius' belief that the way to fix society from the bottom up, not the top down, ultimately had a profound impact on Chinese civilization. Unfortunately, Confucius died before many of these changes took root, and he died thinking he had failed. But certainly, we can all draw inspiration from his insight and his dedication to his principles.

Both Taoism and Confucianism developed both a mass-oriented popular expression and a more narrow and demanding discipline that attracted those who were more spiritually motivated. The good thing about the popular expressions of these faiths is that the pure teaching is made more accessible to the many through the inclusion of various forms of primitive folk religion. This means the faith can help a greater number of people grow both spiritually and ethically. On the other hand, the purity of these traditions became watered down—some might even say polluted—in the attempt to reach greater numbers of people (and to win favors from the powerful and rich, who were in control). In addition, each faith fragmented into hundreds of movements and sects, each with its own unique teaching on how best to return to the power and purity of the original faith.

This struggle between the original pristine motivation of a small, dedicated group of believers and the later growth and development of the movements they founded is one of the recurring themes of the story of humanity's religious impulse. In the process of broadening their outreach, many faiths have incorporated earlier forms of superstition and polytheism. In addition, as faiths evolve and become institutionalized, they become vulnerable to elitism and exclusivity, which can lead to authoritarianism and abuse. And often, fierce forms of fundamentalism arise, often designed to return the faith to its pristine roots.

Each of these faiths is unique, but they all speak of humanity's longing for God.

## THE CHRISTIAN AND OTHER FAITHS

As a Christian, how does one deal with this profusion of religions, each with its own prescriptions for enlightenment and rebirth?

Jesus told his disciples, "I am the way and the truth and the life. No one comes to the Father except through me" (JOHN 14:6). During the past twenty centuries, this passage has inspired millions of Christian missionaries, evangelists, and next-door neighbors to speak to others about their faith.

The same passage from John also includes Jesus' warning about false teachers and prophets who would delude people and divert them from the true path of God. Instead of being good shepherds, Jesus said such people were thieves and robbers. What, then, are we to make of other faiths and teachers, many of which disagree with the teachings of Christianity? Are they, as some have said, spiritual counterfeits inspired by angels of darkness disguised as angels of light? Are they substandard religions that can be abandoned in the light of Christ?

In centuries past, Catholics were unfortunately among the ring-leaders of religious crusading and persecution. In recent centuries, the Church has formally repented of these earlier excesses. And since Vatican II, a series of groundbreaking Catholic meetings held from 1963 to 1966, the Church announced an approach to religious diversity that is more sensitive to our increasingly global under-standing of the human family, an understanding brought about by mass communication and our "shrinking," pluralistic world.

The Church affirmed that Jesus is the fullness of God's revela-tion to humanity, and that the Church is the fullest instrument of God's salvation. The Church also said, however, that all other re-ligions and philosophies participate in the truth of God and in the Spirit of God to the degree that they share in God's truth.

It's important for us to understand that the Church teaches that the work of Christ on the cross extends outward throughout the world, and both forward and backward in time, to provide re-demption to any and all who believe. This may include those who are not followers of Christ but who hear or experience the truth Christ teaches within the context of their own religions and faiths. This would include, for example, faithful Jews who lived during Old Testament times and who never had the opportunity to un-derstand Christianity or reach out in faith to Christ. Present-day Jews at least have the opportunity to know about Christ. (In later chapters we will talk in more detail about Christ, his life, his message, his sacrificial death on a cross for all humanity, and his Resurrection from the dead.)

This all sounds so complex, but it's extremely important. Let me try to explain it with a story.

Suppose you are on a long journey—possibly across Europe—and you are traveling by train. Along the way, you meet a fellow passenger, and during the rest of the journey you and your companion share the joys of the journey, the long hours of conversation, the friendly fellowship of meals and drinks, the beauty of the passing countryside, and the stillness of the dark and quiet night. During your time together, you and your new friend "break through" the barriers that usually separate us from one another to the infinite and eternal you encounter within each other. But when the trip is over, you must part and say goodbye.

Now suppose that you never got your new friend's full name, address, or phone number. Does that mean you didn't have a real and powerful encounter with the person who had been your companion for so many days and hours? Of course not! Even though you don't know all the particulars, you and your travel companion truly experienced an intimacy, openness, and oneness. Your relationship, though incomplete, was real and deep.

Vatican II and subsequent church encyclicals teach us that it's the same with Hindus, Buddhists, Taoists, Platonists, neo-pagans, and others who seek after spiritual truth. They may not know Jesus, or consciously follow him, but they experience him regardless. Theologian Karl Rahner even called them "anonymous Christians." Though they don't read the Bible or belong to a church, some of them exhibit the virtues of the Christian lifestyle more thoroughly than some who do call themselves Christians.

In the past, Christians have often said "no" to other religions. Then we said "yes, but." Today, we have actually returned to a more ancient approach of the early Church by saying "yes, and." This is not the same as "yes," which would degenerate into a universalism that does not accurately portray authentic traditional Christianity, or win the real respect of other traditional world religions. It does, however, take us from a militaristic attitude to a more welcoming and respectful attitude, which both makes us more friendly to others and more peaceful within ourselves.

For me, the chart below is helpful:

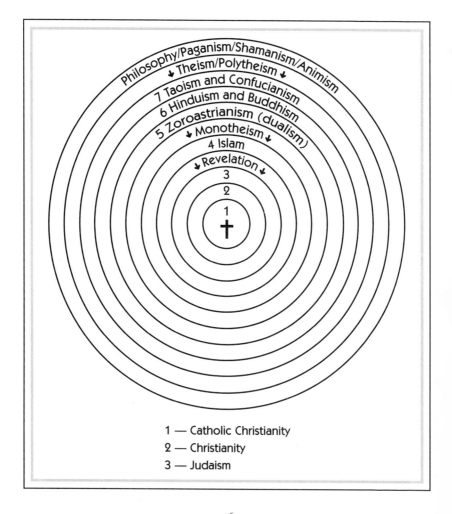

1 — Catholic Christianity
2 — Christianity
3 — Judaism

At the heart of it all is Jesus Christ and Catholic Christianity. Extending out from this central core is what the Bible calls "the body of Christ," which represents all forms of Christianity, including the Protestant, Orthodox, and Anglican traditions. In the next circle is the Jewish faith, which received direct, formal revelation from God in the Hebrew scriptures, also known as the Old Testament.

Followers of Islam believe in many parts of the Old Testament, and much of their faith is inspired by God. Muslims, Jews, and Christians hold a special place, since theirs are the three great monotheistic faiths of the world.

Beyond these monotheistic faiths are a variety of polytheistic religions, philosophies, and primitive practices.

## IT'S NOT ONLY WHAT YOU KNOW, BUT WHERE YOU'RE HEADED

THIS CHART makes everything appear simple, solid, and static. In reality, though, there is continual movement, both inward and outward, as people take different paths on their search to know God.

Interestingly, the word the Bible uses to describe how we can "know" (*eido*) God is the same Greek word that is used to describe the deepest intimacy between husband and wife. In Genesis, for example, Adam is described as "knowing" Eve and procreating children. This is a profound mystery of the faith. The type of relationship God desires us to have with him is not all intellectual head knowledge—as important as that is as a guide—but intimate, personal, and passionate experience of his divine nature. God wants us to know him deeply and personally. Knowing God is deep, mystical, and intimate. It is complete, and involves our entire being—body, soul, and spirit.

One can begin the spiritual quest anywhere, even at the far

edges of the circle. The Church teaches that philosophers or poly-theists can truly know at least some aspects of God. The important thing is that we are moving toward the center. If we are moving in-ward, growing closer to Christ, then we are inspired by the Spirit and experiencing salvation in and through Christ. At each moment in our lives, we face the choice: Follow the Spirit and go for-ward, or turn from the Spirit and go backwards. One is salvation; the other is not. One is life; the other is stagnation and death.

On the other hand, we can be at the very center of the circle, but if we are moving away from the Christ and the core, we are turning our backs on God, Jesus, and salvation. Two people could be at the same point on the chart, yet one may be "saved" and the other damned. One person can even be closer to the center than another and still be more in danger of losing his salvation than someone farther out. It depends on which direction each person is going in. One can be growing in life; the other may be headed to death. The important question is whether we are moving toward or away from the heart of God.

It would be best if everyone could read the words of Jesus in the New Testament and enjoy an individual experience of his person, as I myself did when I was desperately searching for the truth. In my quest for God, I had looked in many places, traditions, rituals, and sacred books. But I eventually discovered that only by reading the words of Jesus and having an experience of his person at the same time can we know God through both Word and Spirit.

Coming to Christ does not always happen this way, however.

As with the story about the two travelers on the train, one can have real and intimate knowledge of another without knowing all the particulars. In other words, one can know through Spirit with-out knowing through the Word. Those who don't hear the Christian message proclaimed can still receive the message of Christ through the work of the Holy Spirit writing that Word on their hearts. In this case, they experience salvation without the specific message of the Gospel of Jesus Christ having ever been given to them.

The Church teaches that ultimately we must receive both Word and Spirit to have the full message of the Gospel of Jesus Christ. But this is a very mystical and personal thing that is really only known to God and God alone. For us to judge others is a dangerous thing indeed, and it's something Jesus warns us against. Judging the spirituality of others leads to presumption, pride, and arrogance, not the love Jesus showed us and desires us to show to others.

In addition to sharing the love of God, though, I am compelled to share the message of God. To do otherwise is also dangerous. Silence about the Word of God can deprive hungry souls who are truly ready to hear of the rich spiritual feast God wants to give them.

The book of Sirach says, there is balance between speaking and listening that we all must find. "Be swift to hear, but slow to answer," writes Sirach. But in another place, the teacher writes, "Refrain not from speaking at the proper time." Or as Saint Peter put it in his epistle:

"Always be ready to give an explanation to anyone who asks you for a reason for your hope, but do it with gentleness and reverence" (1 PETER 3:15–16).

For me, this approach works well. It maintains the absolute and unique centrality of Jesus and the fullness of God's revelation in Christ and his work upon the cross. At the same time, it also takes into account the very real spiritual experiences of faithful, holy, and spiritually advanced men and women within other faiths. It maintains orthodox Christianity without excluding all other religions; and it embraces other religions without reducing Christianity, as many do, to merely another generic, universalistic, feel-good spirituality. This approach recognizes the important cultural, sociological, geographical, and even personal needs different people have for different types of religious expressions. Jesus Christ is presented as absolutely unique, yet not to the exclusion of other religions or faiths.

## THE WAY OF MEDITATION

ONE ASPECT many Westerners find appealing about Eastern religions is their approach to meditation. Most Christians do not give this spiritual practice the importance it deserves. Hinduism, Buddhism, and Taoism all have an ancient, well-developed, and practical approach to the mechanics of meditation that many people, including those who don't subscribe to these faiths, have found very helpful in their own meditation practices.

Christianity does have its own rich tradition of contemplative and mystical spiritual practices. The roots of this tradition can be seen in the monastic and contemplative practices of both the Christian West and East, and found in the writings of the Desert Fathers and Mothers and the Orthodox monastic saints, and in such western mystics as Saint Benedict of Nursia, Saint Bernard of Clairvaux, and Saint Francis of Assisi, to name just a few. I myself am a part of that tradition. At our hermitage in the Ozarks, I and others follow centuries-old practices that bring us together for prayer in the morning, at noon, and in the evening, in addition to our personal prayer throughout the day.

But by and large, many branches of Christianity don't explore meditation as they could. Part of this is due to our Western tendency to describe the "what" but not "how" of a thing. If you look at most sermons, religious books, and seminars, you see that they are full of accurate technical information but they don't take people inside the faith they are talking about. This leaves people stuck in the state of duality and separation Jewish thinker Martin Buber referred to as "I-and-Thou." Instead of breaking through to the mystical reality of God, people are left on the outside looking in. As a result, many believers know a lot about God but few say they regularly sense a direct, personal connection to God.

Many of the Eastern religions explore the "how" of connecting to the divine in precise detail. Though the exact methods differ from one religion and sect to another, there remains a significant agreement about three key areas. These areas are moral precepts, disciplines of the body, and disciplines of the mind.

The *moral precepts and vows* usually deal with matters of right and wrong. Typically, there are injunctions against killing and brutality, lying or harsh words, stealing or selfish actions, unchastity in thought or action, intoxication, and other forms of bodily uncleanness or addiction. Such precepts illustrate the truth that spiritual practice cannot be divorced from the rest of life. Or as many gurus express it, any meditation that is not prepared for through a disciplined and holy life is false. This approach resonates deeply with Christian teachings on holy living.

*Bodily discipline* refers here to the importance of having a proper posture for meditation. In the East, the most common posture has traditionally been the lotus, or cross-legged position. There's nothing supernatural about this posture. It is simply intended to ensure rest and stability during long periods of meditation, so that the body will not cramp or tire prematurely and thus limit the meditation itself. But today, many people who practice meditation sit in a chair, with their back straight and upright and their feet flat on the floor. Directives are also given for the eyes, the tongue, and hands.

Attention is also given to breathing. During periods of meditation, we can go without food or water, but we can't survive without breathing. There are exercises that teach us how to focus on our breathing mentally so that our mind and spirit don't get distracted. Proper breathing helps us let go and focus in on God.

The *disciplines of the mind* are also extremely important, even though some people portray meditation as mindless. Meditation is not mindless; it helps us transcend the mind and leads us to pure intuition or spirit. This requires a stilling of the mind, but without allowing it to wander into aimlessness, which often leads to delusion.

I and many other Catholic Christians practice a form of Christian meditation that incorporates certain aspects of Eastern meditation techniques but without embracing their specific theology.

Surprisingly, many people are unaware of the deep, ancient Catholic monastic and contemplative tradition of which I am a part. This tradition has clear precepts and lifestyle commandments that prepare the whole being for a life of meditation and prayer. We also speak of postures such as bowing, kneeling, sitting, or standing (though postures are not emphasized as much as they are in the East), and environments, such as solitude and silence. There are also ancient Christian breath prayers, and we will discuss one of these soon. All of these Christian contemplative practices are designed to help us transcend thoughts, desires, distractions, and emotions.

What makes the Christian approach to meditation unique is that it is part of a personal love relationship with Jesus Christ. For me, meditation is not merely a mental exercise but a doorway to deeper communion with the living God. For me, the contemplative experience that is beyond activity, words, feelings, or images is only one part of a full relationship with Jesus, but it is the very essence of that relationship.

Meditation isn't easy. It takes dedication and devotion. Some of these disciplines may seem uncomfortable at first because our bodies, minds, and emotions are used to undisciplined, unrestrained, or just plain ineffective habits and lifestyles. But once we go past the initial newness, curiosity, and discomfort of these practices, we can discover that body, emotions, and mind begin to calm, find peace, and finally break through in an experience of enlightenment that can only be described as spiritual rebirth. It actually does work.

## THE WAY OF PRAYER

IF YOU WOULD LIKE to try one of these practices yourself, there are two techniques you can try.

One is the ancient *Jesus Prayer,* which comes down to us through the centuries from the Orthodox Christian East. It works like this:

First, find a calm, quiet area and sit in a still, comfortable posture. Breathe in, and as you do so, say these words:

"Lord Jesus Christ."

Next, breathe out, and as you do so, say these words:

"Have mercy on me, a sinner."

At first, this exercise may seem silly. But as you work on it (these are spiritual *disciplines,* after all), you will find that it calms the body by establishing a deep, natural physical rhythm based on your breathing. Steady breathing also brings oxygen to the blood, organs, and brain.

Praying the Jesus Prayer also focuses the mind on the simple but powerful message of the prayer itself, leaving little room for other speculation or conceptualization. This makes the mind freer for guided meditation on positive spiritual images without distraction. This calming and directing of body and mind, in turn, bring disordered and wild emotions back into harmony, so that they can be used in a constructive manner for ourselves and others. At this point, the rich, mystical theology contained in the words of the prayer is simply intuited in the spirit with each breath. With prayer, you can almost feel the tyranny of disordered emotions fall away and back into their proper place with each breath.

This simple exercise can lead us to the place of breakthrough, where the intuition of pure spirit is set free and reborn in a way that permeates and enlightens body, emotions, and mind. Then all is made new in All. All is born again. With the very rhythm of each breath, your whole being—body, soul, and spirit—intuitively comes back into harmony with the very rhythm and original music of God, humanity, and all creation in a way far beyond concept or speculative thought. It is pure intuition and experience. It is en-lightenment and rebirth.

A second practical technique is the *breath prayer*, which inte-grates Eastern meditation techniques in a way that is consistent with authentic Christian theology.

First, find a quiet place where you won't be distracted, and be seated in a stable and comfortable position, one that won't cause pain or cramp if you maintain it for twenty minutes or more. Sitting can symbolize our humility before Jesus, our teacher, or it can sym-bolize our own authority and stability.

Place your hands in your lap so that they are both comfortable and fixed. You don't want to be interrupted by fidgeting. As for hand position, there's a tradition that says "palms down" means calmness, and "palms up" means openness to God.

Your eyes should be neither closed (which causes sleep, unless you focus on a particular mental image, which is sometimes ad-vised) nor wide open (too many external images will distract you). Rather, do as the masters do. They have their eyes partially open, enabling them to "gaze into infinity." The tongue rests gently be-hind the upper front teeth on the roof of the mouth to keep from nervous swallowing and the like.

Next comes the breath which, as we have seen, is the same word in the Bible as the word for spirit. The goal of breath prayer is to breathe in the Spirit of God, who gives life to both the spirit and the body. Through breath prayer, you can experience union with God and creation by simply "being" in God through Christ.

Breathe deeply yet gently. Breathe from the stomach—or navel—to the depth of your body, which brings life-renewing oxygen into your bloodstream and spreads health throughout. Practice awareness of your own body—an awareness that is a wonderful gift from God. Allow this awareness to grow deeper with each breath. And as you breathe deeply, you may begin to have a heightened sense of your connection to all of creation. At the same time, exhaling symbolizes our letting go of our *body*, which in its present, limited form is impermanent.

As you practice the breath prayer, you may also become more aware of your own *emotions*, which are intimately related to the body, and which unfortunately often control the mind. All of us have emotions, some of which are healthy and some of which aren't. But as you breathe in, acknowledge how you feel at the present moment in time. And as you exhale, let these emotions go, allowing them to find their proper place in serving the soul and energizing the body.

The same could be said concerning *thoughts* that rarely focus well on the eternal things of God, or enter into the more classical passive Christian contemplation beyond all thought, image, and form. As scripture says, "My thoughts are not your thoughts."

I have found, after years of practice, that my breathing during prayer has become deeper and finer, not more shallow and coarse. I have also found that this deeper kind of breathing becomes more natural throughout the day, helping me maintain continual contact with God and counteracting the stress that sneaks up on us all.

These simple exercises are kind of a Contemplation 101. But they work, and they can lead the mind to a breakthrough that per-

meates and enlightens body, emotions, and mind, bringing enlightenment and rebirth. Through practices of this kind, your whole
being—body, soul, and spirit—intuitively comes back into harmony with the original music of God.

## LIVING AND LEARNING

SINCE THE 1960s, the Catholic church has emphasized the importance of real dialogue between Catholic Christians and those
people who are members of other Christian bodies or other world
religions. All around the world, groups of believers, including pas-
tors and theologians, have been getting together to talk about their
faith and learn about the faith of others.

Those who have participated in these gatherings have discovered that the whole process really doesn't work unless it is mutual,
and it can't be mutual if one party is convinced its side has all the
answers. When someone takes the know-it-all approach, the result
isn't dialogue; it's debate, or an effort to convert others to your
views. I think it's fine to evangelize—to share your faith with others—but not when participating in a dialogue.

Dialogue doesn't mean compromising your beliefs or caving in
to others. In fact, the best communication between people of different faiths happens when everyone is prepared and sure of his or
her own position, but at the same time curious and humble enough
to learn from someone else. That's the approach I take when I come
into contact with people of other faiths.

I am utterly convinced of the truth of Jesus' words: that he is the
way, the truth, and the life. I also believe that Jesus represents the
fullness of God's revelation to humanity. But that doesn't mean I
have to be prideful and combative when I talk to others who believe differently.

God is a giver of many gifts. In addition to the many gifts he has given Catholic Christians, he has bestowed many gracious blessings on other Christian believers. Of course, Christians do not always use the gifts of God very well. Some we don't even use at all anymore. They just sit around and collect dust on our church gift shelf.

God has given many other beautiful gifts to Buddhists, Hindus, pagans, and other believers, and some of them might well use a gift that we Christians have, but have neglected.

I can learn much about my gifts by seeing how others use the gifts God has given them. They might have an insight or practice that is far superior to mine. But since I am confident about my relationship to Jesus, I am not intimidated by another's success or superiority in using that gift.

In the end, it all becomes a humble sharing of our blessings, the lessons we've learned, and our strengths, all of it helping us to achieve the one thing that is most important in life: growing stronger spiritually and moving toward the center of the circle of God.

# The Revelation of God

THE QUEST FOR GOD — OR NATURAL RELIGION — IS HUMANITY reaching for God. In that inspired longing, it becomes difficult to say absolutely if the reality we have grasped is God or not. Beyond the desire for beauty, justice, and truth, it gets confusing as we try to determine how these things express themselves in tangible ways. Sometimes, life needs, even demands, something more concrete.

Each one of us has received at least a small portion of the music of God in our souls. We all have been created in God's image, and as a result we inherently desire to create the music of the cosmos with our divine Creator. But no one grasps God in God's entirety. We are limited and finite; only God is eternal and infinite. Therefore, each of us is at least partially deaf to the music of God.

Our spiritual vision is blurred. All of us, as the Apostle Paul wrote, "see through a glass darkly."

We are not all-knowing; only God is. Therefore, we may indeed discover something of absolute truth, but we cannot say absolutely if it is absolute or not. Philosophers call this the problem of epistemology, or the question of how we know what we know. The Catholic Church recognizes some truth in what all philosophies and natural religions say about God or the things of God, but we also hold that Jesus is the fullness of God's Revelation, and that Catholic Christians have been given the fullest and most abundant experience of salvation for those who choose to plumb its depths.

Still, different faiths propose differing definitions of God and varying prescriptions for how we should live our spiritual lives. Unfortunately, beyond the desires we all have for beauty, justice, and truth, it's often difficult to determine who is speaking the truth about God and who is merely living in delusion.

French existentialist philosopher Jean-Paul Sartre once put it like this: "A finite point has no meaning without an infinite reference point." Today it's trendy for people to say, "I have my truth, and you have your truth." Of course, it can be morning in New York while it's evening in Calcutta. And obviously, each of us perceives things differently. But beyond the particularities of our own experiences, there must be some kind of overarching reference point. Philosophers, scientists, and theologians, through much of human history, have been engaged in the intense search for an absolute reference point.

Over the millennia that humans have lived on the earth, our search never uncovered the existence of this absolute reference point. But what we were unable to find, God revealed to us. This process of God revealing himself to us is one of the most important concepts in the entire Judeo-Christian tradition: the concept called Revelation.

In the last chapter, on natural religion, we talked about humanity's quest for God. This refers to our reaching out for God. But Revelation refers to the process of God reaching to us in an extraordinary way, showing and disclosing himself and his wisdom to us in clear and understandable ways. In natural religion, we reach for God. In Revelation, God reaches back in a special way.

## THE UNFOLDING STORY

OVER THE CENTURIES, the Revelation of God to humanity has grown more complete. It's as if over the successive centuries, we have become ready to learn more of what God has to show us.

God revealed important things to Adam, Noah, and then Abraham—three patriarchs who are revered by Jews, Muslims, and Christians. None of these Revelations was complete or exhaustive, but each gave humanity a little more reliable information about the nature of God and reality. The grand unveiling came to Moses, a man with whom God conversed at such great length that Moses' face shown with divine glory, and he had to be veiled when he spoke to the people of Israel. No other Jewish prophet or sage would have such a direct and powerful mystical experience of God until the time of Christ.

God had already called his special people—the Jews—through Abraham, Jacob, and Joseph. Over time, the Jews became guests and then slaves in Egypt, where their sense of religious monotheism was developing, through God's guidance.

God used Moses and miracles to deliver the Jews from Egyptian slavery. First, God spoke to Moses at the site of the burning bush—which burned but was not consumed. Then came a series of plagues that helped persuade Pharaoh to let the Jews go. Next came the angel of death that "passed over" the Jewish people on that great and terrible last night in Egypt, a night now honored by Jews as the Passover. And once the Jews had left Egypt to begin their exodus to the Promised Land, there was the pillar of cloud that led them by day, and the pillar of fire that showed the way by night.

All these miracles were marvelous, but the most amazing thing was when God called Moses up out of the desert and onto Mount Sinai. There, God gave us the Law, writing the Ten Commandments supernaturally with his own finger. Nobody really knows exactly how this happened. We only know that God gave the Ten Commandments to humanity directly from himself in an unprecedented act of Revelation. There was no human mediator, as was typical in the case of holy men or prophets who occasionally spoke for God. This was directly from God, straight from the source.

This act gave the Jews—and gives us today—an absolute, unquestionable reference point for understanding and relating to the One God, the Creator and sustainer of the cosmos. Before this event, many people in many lands had created numerous descriptions of God, but God had never spoken so clearly for himself. No one had ever had this kind of direct divine Revelation before.

The Revelation that came to Moses on Mount Sinai was not a vision or a voice that some guru or holy man claimed was from God. Rather, this was a tablet of stone, spelling out our duties to God and to one another, engraved by God's own finger.

But this meeting on Mount Sinai was not the end of God's Revelation to us. It was just the beginning. Down through the centuries God sent men and women as prophets to communicate with us. Interestingly, each one of these divine spokespeople presented the message of God in a way that reflected his or her own unique personality. God doesn't obliterate our personalities and our uniqueness, turning us into religious robots. Instead, he uses the uniqueness of our lives to achieve his ends, if we will cooperate.

## TRUTH IS NOT ENOUGH

HOW MANY TIMES have you heard people enmeshed in one of life's many messes say, "If only I knew what God wanted me to do right now!"

Ironically, through Revelation the Jews finally knew exactly what God wanted from them, but this still wasn't enough to help them do what was right.

The whole extraordinary history of the Jewish people can be seen as a series of cycles, alternating between sin and salvation, rebellion and redemption. They sin, are punished, and are forgiven over and over. The sins of Moses and the whole first generation of Jews who left Egypt were so severe that they all died without reaching the Promised Land. Instead, Joshua led the next generation to their new home.

Then, after many years of theocratic rule, the Jewish people decide they want a king so they can be like other nations. They get a king, Saul, who begins as a good ruler but quickly goes bad. Then they get another, David, whom the Bible describes as "a man after God's own heart." But even he falls away and must turn back to God for forgiveness in his twilight years. Then Solomon, who was widely hailed as the wisest man on earth, rules with God's own special gift of wisdom. But after a time, he turns away from God to worship false gods.

And so it goes. Good and bad, up and down. The Jews enjoy social unity, then experience a divided kingdom with separate kings in Judah and Israel. Finally, they turn their back on God and are carried off into captivity. After this total humiliation, God gathers them back to the Holy Land to rebuild their temple in the city of

Jerusalem, returning the whole nation to at least a degree of dignity and self-determination once again.

Even then, they wavered once more, relying less on God and increasingly playing politics with nearby empires before they wound up as a small province in the mighty Roman Empire, with a fraction of the glory they once enjoyed. Through it all, the Jews knew exactly what God wanted them to do, thanks to the Law and to a string of prophets who delivered God's messages and called his people back to spiritual purity once again.

Of course, there was always a small remnant that closely followed God's revealed will. But most blindly followed their passions, or the lure of other gods. They knew the Law but wouldn't—or couldn't—obey it. Clearly, something else was needed besides the Law God had inscribed on Moses' stone tablets. But what could this greater Revelation be?

## WORD BECOMES FLESH

TWO THOUSAND YEARS AGO, Jesus came to us as God Incarnate. Law became Love. Word became flesh. Truth became a transforming power that enabled anyone who really desired it to follow God's will.

This further Revelation necessary for the success of salvation for God's people and all humankind was the Incarnation. This word comes from the root "carne," which means "flesh" or "meat." It means literally that the word of God's Revelation takes on flesh. Incarnation means that through Jesus, who was the Son of God, the word of God's Revelation takes on human flesh. Or as John put it in his Gospel:

*In the beginning was the Word,*
*and the Word was with God,*

*and the Word was God. . . .*
*And the Word became flesh*
*and made his dwelling among us* [JOHN 1:1, 14].

Jesus didn't try to force us to live the Law of God. Instead, he told all who heard him, "You must be born again." (Or as other translations put it, "born from above," or "born of the Spirit.") Here we come back to the language of the childhood and innocence. Humanity has strayed. Life has become violent, brutal, and aggressive. Humanity has splintered into warring groups of nations with different languages and religions. In short, we have totally forgotten about the original child God had created us to be. And Jesus comes to help us be born again—to be children once more.

People had searched for God from the beginning of time, building ancient stone monuments and practicing esoteric rituals to commune with the divine. In time, God reached back in an extraordinary way through Revelation, communicating to us through the Law, the prophets, and the wisdom of the books we now call the Old Testament.

Then, at an instant biblical writers call "the fullness of time," God himself took on flesh in the form of Christ, dwelling among us through the Incarnation. Jesus' life, words, and deeds make up much of the books called the New Testament.

Some have attempted to explain the difference between the Old and New Testaments this way: In the Old Testament, God wrote us a letter. This letter was truly written by God's own hand, but it was composed and sent to us from far, far away. But in the New Testament, God pays us a personal visit in Jesus. Through Jesus, God comes close, very close to us. He comes right into our world. He comes right into our own lives. He comes right into our heart, mind, and soul.

Or as the Apostle Paul explained it, the Old Testament was a "schoolmaster" or "tutor" to prepare us for the full and unique Revelation of Christ.

This radical, revolutionary transition—from a word written on tablets of stone, sheepskin, and papyrus to a word written in human flesh—shows the love God has for us. In an effort to break down the barriers between us and God, God steps into our lives, incorporating his life right into the midst of ordinary human life.

God's word is no longer static and cold, delivered to us on top of a high mountain, shrouded in a mystery of cloud, fire, and smoke. Now God's word is dynamic and close. It is living and real.

In Jesus, we can see exactly how God's law is to be lived out. Through his supreme example, we can clearly see how we are to "flesh out," or incarnate, the life God wants us to live. For example, in his Sermon on the Mount, Jesus repeatedly cites the law of Moses, but he also amends the law, teaching by word and example about the inner spirit and motivation behind the law. Where the Old Testament had said there should be "an eye for eye, and a tooth for a tooth," Jesus teaches us to go beyond this law of equivalency and turn the other cheek, thus emphasizing that God's original purpose was mercy, not retribution or seeking revenge. In the process, God's Word expands in dynamism and mystery, yet it is made more understandable and believable. It is a more complete Revelation. It is Incarnation.

This is why in Catholic Christian churches of the New Covenant, we now house the Blessed Sacrament in a receptacle called a tabernacle. In the Jewish synagogue, the tabernacle was the place in which the Scriptures were housed. Christian pilgrims who visit the Holy Land can view these tabernacles in the symbolic "tomb of David" below the Upper Room where the Eucharist was instituted by Jesus, the new David. The pilgrims often say, "Why does the Jewish tabernacle look like our tabernacle?"

Actually, it is ours that looks like theirs! We continue using the tabernacle of the Jewish synagogue and keep it within our Christian churches. Only now it no longer houses only a written word. It houses an Incarnate Word. A Word that is a "mystery," or a "sacrament." We still honor the written Word. We enthrone the Scriptures with special honor and quote them abundantly at every liturgy. But the tabernacle now is for the mystical, or sacramental, presence of Jesus, the Incarnate Word, the living Word, the Word made flesh and dwelling among us in the people of God, the church.

Jesus confirms everything written in the Law and spoken by the prophets. But he also reveals more, so much more, than God could show us through words alone. We honor the old Revelation but embrace the new Revelation—the Incarnation of God.

## BRIDGING HUMAN AND DIVINE

WE WILL TALK MORE about Jesus in the next chapter, but for now, there's one other important point we need to make about the uniqueness of Incarnation. For Jesus represents God in a way that no one else has ever done in all of human history.

Nearly all of the mystics and sages of every major world religion have spoken in paradoxes. They taught that we could find new life in death, wealth in poverty, fulfillment in renunciation, and so on. But in the case of Jesus, he not only taught and exhibited these things, he lived them to the point of death—death on a cross—and more impressively, he rose from the dead on the third day. No other religious founder, prophet, or alleged incarnation of God has ever manifested these paradoxes in such a clear and unquestionable way through his own life.

All religions have their prophets and avatars. These are men and women believed to be the representatives or spokespeople of the gods. This is a beautiful belief, and an important part of human history. But such people are not the same thing as what Christian belief describes when it talks about the Incarnation of Christ. For Jesus is the full and unique manifestation of God for all time.

When God spoke to Moses from the burning bush, Moses asked God what his name was, and God replied, "I AM that I AM." All peoples and religions seek the knowable and the unknowable, the personal and the transpersonal, the practical and the mystical aspects of the divine. The unknowable, transpersonal, and mystical aspects of God are awesomely revealed to the Jews in the Old Testament.

In an extraordinary way, Jesus called himself the "I AM." This is the most exalted language that can be used, and Jesus uses it to describe himself. He is seen and beyond our seeing; known yet beyond mere knowledge; clear yet mysterious; human yet divine—all in one expression of Incarnation. This is the perfect theological and mystical balance, yet it is still something so awesome that it eludes all logic and wisdom.

Another time, Jesus told the Apostle Thomas that anyone who has seen Jesus "has seen the Father." Later, Jesus commands his apostles to baptize people in the name of the Father, the Son, and the Holy Spirit, implying that Jesus himself is a coequal part of God.

The New Testament is clear on the uniqueness and the divinity of Jesus. One famous passage states:

He is the image of the invisible God,
the firstborn of all creation.
For in him were created all things in heaven and on earth,
the visible and the invisible,
whether thrones or dominions or principalities or powers;
all things were created through him and for him.
He is before all things,
and in him all things hold together [COLOSSIANS 1:15–17].

Another passage, this one geared to Jewish readers, said:

> In times past, God spoke in partial and various ways to our
> ancestors through the prophets; in these last days, he spoke to us
> through a son, whom he made heir of all things and through whom
> he created the universe,
> who is the refulgence of his glory,
> the very imprint of his being,
> and who sustains all things by his mighty word
> [HEBREWS 1:1–3].

I could include many other similar passages here, but the point
is clear. Jesus is utterly unique, and his ministry is described as "once
and for all." As Jesus himself says at one point, "I am the way and
the truth and the life. No one comes to the Father except through
me" (JOHN 14:6).

As a Christian, I deny nothing in other faiths that is beautiful,
good, and true, for all beauty, goodness, and truth come from God
and lead back to God. Indeed, I applaud all people of faith and join
them in our common search for and experience of God. But at the
same time, I must make it clear that I understand Jesus to be the full
and unique expression of God. (The Buddhists, for example, refer
to both Jesus and Buddha as "Awakened Ones." But as a Christian,
I believe that if the Buddha is awake, it is ultimately because Jesus
woke him.)

To some, this may sound judgmental or exclusivist, but that's
certainly not the purpose. Christians through the ages have sought
to embrace and endorse all that is good and true in the world's
many philosophies and religions. We seek to stand humbly on common ground with all who seek things divine.

But Christians are unlike those who believe there are many

gods, or many incarnations of God. For example, we are different from Buddhists, who believe that all religions, including their own, are only "fingers pointing to the moon." Christians believe that Jesus is a unique and unrepeatable Incarnation of the one, true God. Jesus is not a finger pointing at the moon; he *is* the moon. Better yet: Jesus is the sun who illumines the moon.

The Dalai Lama recently spoke to a gathering of Christians, and he said three profound things:

First, he emphasized that the uniqueness of every religious tradition is to be preserved and respected. Trying to blend all the world's faiths together into some kind of one-size-fits-all universalism is dishonest. It is like trying to put a camel's head on a yak's body.

Second, the Dalai Lama acknowledged that even though he does not personally believe in the Christian doctrine of the Incarnation, he does believe that Jesus is a Buddha, or an Awakened One, who is one of many incarnations of the divine. And the Dalai Lama expressed his respect for Christians' belief in the uniqueness of Jesus, since this a central teaching of the Christian faith, and should be respected as such.

Finally, this man who is one of the world's most respected religious leaders challenged his Christian listeners not to try winning over other believers through argument or debate but through taking the lead in the global struggle for spirituality, peace, and justice. People are rarely persuaded by argument, he said, but are more deeply moved by seeing someone live out their faith with integrity and compassion. I find his words challenging indeed.

Catholic Christianity claims to follow Jesus, who is unique among all the other world's religions, gods, and incarnations. Through Jesus, God has given us the fullness of his gifts, but unfortunately, we don't always use those gifts in ways that serve all humanity and creation in the best way. Often, other traditions use the gifts God has given them much more effectively than we do. This means Christians still have a lot of work to do.

Part of this work involves plumbing the depths of our own tradition, learning its mystical foundations, and practicing its radical lifestyles. But at the same time, we must develop a working knowledge and deep appreciation for the other religious and spiritual traditions of the world.

On both the objective and mystical levels, we must understand the differences and unique gifts of each faith. But we must also appreciate those aspects of our faith traditions that we hold in common, such as the commitment among Christians, Jews, and Muslims to the belief in one God.

As Christians, we will see Jesus as part of and the fulfillment of humanity's much broader spiritual quest. At the same time, we will see Jesus—the unique Incarnation of the Creator God—as the real unifier and fulfillment of all.

# The Real Jesus

WE SEE HIS PICTURE EVERYWHERE: IN ANCIENT CHURCHES and modern sanctuaries; on holy cards and paintings; and even on the cover of *Time* magazine. He is the topic of seminars that bear his name, and heralded as the champion of every new theological theory. He is preached by conservative fundamentalists and liberal liberation fighters. Who is he?

Is Jesus more like Mother Teresa and Saint Francis, or a contemporary television evangelist, "mega-church" pastor, or motivational speaker? Even further, does the real Jesus more resemble the typical Western-style Christianity we see around us today, or would he look more like a Buddhist monk, Hindu holy man, or Taoist sage?

In Jesus' day as in our own, people's perceptions were colored by life experience and other factors. That's the way it was with his apostles, his disciples, and the multitudes who heard him speak. Some loved him, some hated him. Some appreciated him, some resented him. Some were loyal, some betrayed him. Some looked for a holy man or Messiah, some looked for a political and military savior.

Who is the real Jesus? It can be hard to tell. But in our quest to find him, we must look toward two different but overlapping sources: the historical Jesus and the mystical Jesus.

## THE HISTORICAL JESUS

WHO WAS THIS MAN who walked the earth nearly two thousand years ago? Even when he was physically in their midst, the people of Jesus' day didn't quite know what to make of him. His disciples loved him and hung on his every word (except for the one who betrayed him), while the multitudes found him intriguing and entertaining, and the power elites saw him as a frightening rabble rouser and had him put to death.

Death was not the end for this man. Many other holy men and religious teachers had walked the earth, dispensed their wisdom, and died. But Jesus was different. He had said he was the unique Incarnation of God, a claim supported by his Resurrection from the dead three days after he was crucified between two criminals on a crude wooden cross.

What might have happened if Buddha had died and then risen from the dead? Or Gandhi? Or Martin Luther King, Jr.? Their followers would have gone wild with enthusiasm and would have told the world the news. That's precisely what happened with Jesus, and it *only* happened with Jesus.

For members of the early Church, who enthusiastically proclaimed the message of the Resurrection of Jesus, this once-and-for-all miracle provided the foundation for their preaching about the victory of life over death, righteousness over sin, and light over darkness. These followers wrote down many of his words and deeds, and these writings—which we now have in the New Testament—have been passed down to us through the centuries.

## THE MYSTICAL JESUS

WHAT DOES THIS ANCIENT FIGURE mean to us today? As a result of the Resurrection, Jesus is more than a wise man or sage and Christianity is more than a creed. Jesus lives today. We can experience him subjectively and existentially through the gift of his Spirit, the reception of the Sacraments he instituted, prayer and private devotion, and participation in the rich and dynamic life within the body of his people—the Church.

Over the centuries, many creative individuals—some of them sincere and some not so sincere—have concocted extreme legends about Jesus. One popular legend about Jesus is reappearing today after making a big splash in the sixties and seventies—a time when I and many others were desperately seeking God. This is the legend that Jesus was really a Buddhist who had studied for years in Asia. Though interesting in theory, this legend is based less on strong evidence than on the desire for evidence to prove an interesting theory.

In our own time, a group of scholars who have come together under their own authority and call themselves "The Jesus Seminar" suffer from a similar problem with the historical evidence about the life of Christ. Seminar members debate and then vote to decide which parts of the New Testament they believe are authentic and which are unreliable. The group has boldly declared that Jesus didn't do or say most of what the Bible claims he did. Unlike those who make up a "Buddhist Jesus legend," the Jesus Seminar has rejected much solid evidence about the life and teaching about Jesus. In the end, they don't accept much of what the Church and her countless saints found so helpful in their faith and mystical experience.

But we don't have to reject the Church's gospel to find a mystical and radical understanding and life in Christ. The simple New Testament Gospel gives us the facts and teachings of the historical Jesus as recorded by those who knew him best that we need. And our own communication with the living Christ can help us encounter the mystical Jesus in the here and now. In this chapter, we will be relying on these two sources to guide us to the truth of the most important question in the world: Who is the real Jesus?

## IN SEARCH OF THE REAL JESUS

THE NAME "JESUS" is the English version of the name Jeshua, which comes from the Hebrew language (where it shares the same root as the name "Joshua") and means "savior" and "salvation." Jesus is a fairly common name in Latino cultures today, and it was also common in Jesus' day, when many claimed to be a "Christ" (a name which means "Messiah" or "Anointed One"). There were others who claimed to be the Messiah, and some of them even had the name "Jesus." But the Jesus we read about in the New Testament and the salvation he brings us are unique.

What does it mean to be "saved"? Most of us have heard this term so much that we have almost been numbed to its meaning. We associate it with wild-eyed evangelists who come knocking at our front door, or who confront us in airports, demanding to know whether or not we are "saved."

The only people I know who truly understand the meaning of salvation are the people who have nearly lost their lives and know it: people who have been rescued from a burning house, or a sinking boat, or a terrible accident that nearly cost them or a loved one their life. These people understand what it is to be saved. Salvation is literally a rescue.

The Twelve Steps of Alcoholics Anonymous and other recovery programs begin with step number one: admitting that our life is totally unmanageable and out of control without the help of a "Higher Power." For AA's founders, this Higher Power originally meant Jesus. And if you have known any people who have ruined their lives with alcohol, drugs, or addictive behaviors, you can really appreciate what it means to need salvation, or recovery.

The word "salvage" also helps us understand what Jesus means by salvation. In my mind, the term brings up images of a massive, weed-strewn salvage yard filled with old wrecked cars, trucks, tractors, and the like. For many of us, our lives have become wrecks. We are no longer "drivable." We no longer function as the manufacturer intended. We have been broken down and need to be towed to the salvage yard.

Spiritually speaking, God's grace is the tow truck, the Church is the salvage yard, and our brothers and sisters are God's repair workers. Once we arrive there, God begins his work of rebuilding the broken pieces of our lives. He gets rid of the things that can't be repaired, salvages the usable parts, and puts us back together to create something beautiful and new. Often, these rebuilt "salvage jobs" can even turn out better than the originals. It seems miraculous that something so wrecked could come out so perfect and new. Jesus is truly a savior, and the Church, which was established by the real Jesus, is a place that can be redemptive and reparative.

## THE ULTIMATE SACRIFICE

How does God bring salvation to us? Theologians say salvation comes through the vicarious atonement of the cross of Christ. This sounds complex, but its meaning is simple to grasp.

"Vicarious" means "in place of." "Atone" means "to forgive through sacrifice and the shedding of blood." In short, then, vicarious atonement means that we have our sins forgiven by someone else taking our place to receive the just punishment we deserve.

The whole notion of blood sacrifice and atonement may sound very alien to modern ears, but the practice was common throughout much of the ancient world, including the Celts of Britain and the Maya of Mexico.

Why was such sacrifice required in ancient faiths? Because blood is a powerful symbol of life. Primitive peoples clearly understood that blood is important to survival, and they believed that their gods, who were the givers and takers of life, would bless them if they made a blood sacrifice.

Interestingly, "sacrifice" comes from the same root as "sacred." To sacrifice means to give up something for another out of love. Throughout the ages, all faiths have taught that it is very holy to give up something as a sign of love for God. This explains why ascetic disciplines often incorporate fasting or vigils. Although these may be uncomfortable to the worshiper, they help us deny ourselves and the tyranny of our desires, and such sacrifices are pleasing to God.

Atonement by blood sacrifice was an important part of the Jewish rituals that God revealed to his priests and prophets before the time of Christ, and in many ways these rituals anticipate the sacrificial work of Jesus. But atonement in the Judeo-Christian tradition differs significantly from the kinds of sacrifices regularly practiced by ancient pagan people.

For one thing, Hebrew tradition called only for the sacrificing of animals, never human beings. The only possible exception to this rule was the time God tested Abraham, asking him to sacrifice his favorite son, Isaac. But in the end, God delivered an animal, which Abraham sacrificed in place of Isaac.

Another unusual case was the Passover in the book of Exodus. In this case, the blood of lambs was put on the doorposts of Hebrew houses in order that the angel of death would "pass over" their dwellings during the Hebrews' last night in the slavery of Egypt. The angel of death did enter the houses where there was no blood, and as a result, the firstborn child of every Egyptian home was killed. This is the origin of the Jewish Passover meal, which serves as the pattern for the Christian Eucharist, or the Lord's Supper.

Typically, it was precious and spotless animals that were sacrificed. When animals were sacrificed, blood was offered as a symbol of atonement, and the meat was shared with the whole family, with those who served as ministers, and with the poor. Jewish sacrificial practices not only spared human life but also had practical and beneficial effects for humans.

With so many centuries of tradition involving humans offering sacrifices to God, it's extraordinary, then, that the ultimate sacrifice—the sacrifice of Jesus on a cross—was not us making the sacrifice. It began, rather, with God making a sacrifice for us. How astonishing! The one who should receive the sacrifice is offering it for us. In Jesus' humanity, he offers himself to God for us. In his crucifixion on the cross, Jesus becomes both priest and victim, so that we might share in his priesthood and learn how to offer ourselves as well. The divine takes on humanity so that humanity might share in divinity. The vicarious atonement of Christ takes us deep into the mysteries at the heart of God.

In speaking to his disciples, Jesus spoke only briefly and incompletely about his impending crucifixion. But later it was Saint Paul who wrote extensively—and sometimes beautifully—about the sacrifice of Christ. In his effort to communicate the message of Jesus to all the world, Paul often explained the atonement in terms that transcended traditional Jewish understandings of blood sacrifice.

Paul, speaking to a largely Greek audience, Hellenized the

Christian teaching of the atonement. That means he used Greek language and concepts to communicate to a Greek culture. In Paul's hands, the atonement sounded less like a messy religious ritual than it did a legal transaction, with God demanding his own Son's life in exchange for the sins of the human race. Paul eloquently describes how Jesus' infinite grace brings the scales of divine justice into balance, giving all of us the chance to experience his sacrifice made on our behalf.

In recent decades, some critics have claimed that Paul pirated the essentials of Christianity, twisting them (and Hellenizing them) until he created a new religion: "Paulianity." But I think anyone who reads Paul's descriptions of Christ's atoning death will clearly see that he was only attempting to explain this supreme event in a way that would make sense to people who had no background in Jewish traditions.

## A FATHER'S LOVE

FOR ME, the best explanation of what the atonement is all about can be found in a simple illustration from family life.

We can understand the vicarious atonement of Jesus on the cross as similar to a parent who has told his child not to play with his ball in the street. As the parent explains, the child may play anywhere else: in the family's front yard, or in the large park down the street, but not in the street. The street is busy, the father explains, filled with fast-moving cars and trucks, and the drivers don't always look carefully for children. "Do you understand?" asks the parent. "Yes," answers the child.

But soon, in the thrill of play, the son accidentally kicks the ball into the busy street. In an instant, a flash of adrenaline sends the child into the street to retrieve the ball. For that split second, he totally forgets his parent's command. Even if he did remember, the adrenaline rush and the challenge of the chase overpowered parental caution, rendering it null in the child's active mind.

The parent, meanwhile, has been working around the yard, but keeping a watchful eye on his beloved son. Suddenly, he sees the child dart into the street. At the same instant, the parent sees a huge delivery truck speeding down the street and straight toward his child. Without hesitation, the loving parent drops everything and runs into the street, pushing his child out of the way. But having saved his child, he is unable to save himself. The parent is hit by the truck and killed, sacrificing his life to save the one he loved.

So it is with the cross of Christ. Our heavenly father told us what to do to stay out of danger. And at one time, we understood the simple and clear command. Yet in the heat of life, we found ourselves in danger anyway. God saw our predicament from heaven, but instead of judging or abandoning us, he rushed to save us from certain death. Through our own carelessness and stupidity, we placed ourselves in a deadly situation. Yet Jesus pushed us out of harm's way, taking our place in death and freeing us to live again.

This is the true meaning of atonement. This is the message of the Good News of the Gospel. God can do that which we can't— atone for sin and death. But Jesus came back to life after dying in our place. Now we, his disobedient children, are filled with gratitude. From now on, we cling to him in grateful embrace. We listen to his counsel, and obey.

As Jesus once said, "No one has greater love than this, to lay down one's life for one's friends" (JOHN 15:13). Such sacrifice is much more than a mere legal obligation. It is greater than the irrational requirement of some bloody pagan god of stone. Instead, this is the ultimate sacrifice—the greatest manifestation of love the world has ever seen. God is love, and in the atonement, this love manifests itself in life-changing action.

I remember how a monastic brother in our community once

told me about his own experience of God's love. He was out walking the mountain roads and wooded trails that surround our monastic hermitage. Suddenly, he was overcome with a sense that God loved him so much that even if he were the only person on earth, Jesus still would have sacrificed his life to atone for his sins. The brother was overwhelmed, and began to weep tears of gratitude and joy. But mixed with his joy was sadness, for he had turned away from the God who loved him so much.

Thus this dear brother's tears became a mingling of sorrow and joy together. For him, the atonement was no longer a theological abstraction. It was intimate and personal. He knew the vicarious and atoning death of Jesus on the cross was God's ultimate expression of love for *him!* This was more than a legal contract. This was pure self-sacrifice. This was love.

Theology is often where we start in our quest to understand things, but we can't stop there. May we understand the atonement as deeply as this brother did. May we understand this love gift from our heart. May we weep as we are overwhelmed by the paradox that surpasses sorrow or joy in a mystical love union. Then we will understand its real meaning.

## FULLNESS IN EMPTINESS

JESUS CAME TO BRING us salvation, and he also came to show us how to live our lives. And even though his death for us on the cross was a one-time event in history, there's another way we can imitate him in giving ourselves for the sake of God, actualizing the cross of Christ in the here and now.

One of the deepest, most powerful mysteries of the real Jesus is the concept of kenosis, or self-emptying. Jesus emptied himself in his atoning sacrifice, bringing eternal life to all of us through death. This is the paradox of self-emptying: death bringing life. Through self-emptying, we can all find riches in poverty, love in chastity, freedom in obedience, and light in divine darkness. Through his atonement, Christ has confounded opposites. He has gone through and past duality into oneness. It is no longer one through the other; it is one *in* the other.

Saint Paul's letter to the Philippians eloquently describes this important concept:

> . . . *though he was in the form of God,*
> *did not regard equality with God something to be grasped.*
> *Rather, he emptied himself,*
> *taking the form of a slave,*
> *coming in human likeness;*
> *and found human in appearance,*
> *he humbled himself,*
> *becoming obedient to death,*
> *even death on a cross.*
> *Because of this, God greatly exalted him*
> *and bestowed on him the name*
> *that is above every name,*
> *that at the name of Jesus*
> *every knee should bend,*
> *of those in heaven and on earth and under the earth,*
> *and every tongue confess that*
> *Jesus Christ is Lord,*
> *to the glory of God the Father* [PHILIPPIANS 2:6–11].

But it is not only Christians who understand this concept. In fact, the concept of self-emptying is perhaps the greatest common ground Christians share with the mystics and monks of other religions, but without compromising any aspects of our Catholic Christian faith. All major religions teach the mystical doctrine of emptiness. But at the same time, Jesus shows us the path of self-emptying in a very special way.

Taoism describes emptiness most beautifully, as we see in the *Tao-Te Ching*, by Lao-tzu. This spiritual classic says the spokes of a wheel must converge on an empty space before the wheel can be connected to a cart and really be of service. Similarly, a house is a tangible, solid structure, but it is the empty space that is the most useful for actual living. A window is important, but it is the empty space that is most beneficial for those wanting a gentle and refreshing breeze. Vases and jars might be beautiful, but it is the empty space that makes them of real value. The Tao encourages us to "attain to the utmost Emptiness and cling single-heartedly to interior peace."

Buddhists also emphasize emptiness as a virtue, believing that ultimate nirvana is totally living, yet totally empty, both at peace and still. But it might be good to point out here that the Christian concept of self-emptying is not exactly the same as the Buddhist doctrine of "no self." Buddhism emphasizes the impersonal aspect of human essence. Everything in the cosmos—ourselves included—is ultimately seen as impersonal and impermanent, according to Buddhism. The seemingly personal aspects of ourselves and of God are real, but only as they are manifestations of the impersonal Eternal.

Obviously, Christianity's teaching on both the personhood of God and our own personality objectively differs with Buddhism here. For the Christian, the self is real and even eternal, but it is sacrificed and emptied in order to break through to the realm of the spirit beyond all such concepts or words. This breakthrough is beyond description, concepts, emotions, or words. It is pure essence and intuition.

Scripture teaches us of the two great ways Jesus emptied himself for us: the Incarnation and the Cross.

The *Incarnation*, as we discussed in an earlier chapter, reveals the mystical paradox of God's self-emptying. God becomes man without losing his divinity, enabling humanity to share in that divinity. Glory takes on humility as a way to lead all to glory. Light takes on darkness as a way back to the light. Righteousness takes on sin—without becoming sinful—to show the way of righteousness. The full communion with the Trinity takes on the solitude and separation of the fallen human condition in order to lead all back into full communion, or common union, with and in the Trinity.

Thus the path of emptiness is the way to fullness. Darkness is the way to light. Silence is the way to the Word. Solitude is the way to true community. And so goes the paradox into almost every aspect of human life. Self-emptying breaks us through to a mystical dimension, giving us a whole new understanding and experience of reality that is a unity beyond the seeming opposites. It breaks beyond the duality of superficial human existence to a deeper level of truth where we find pure union with the divine.

The *cross* is the second—and most exalted—way Jesus shows us the paradox of self-emptying. Here self-emptying is raised up for all to see. It becomes the clearest single religious symbol of the path of self-emptying, which all mystics of all religions seek and preach. It is paradox exalted. It is self-emptying clearly defined. It is an action in the ceasing of action and a proclaimed Word in final and complete silence. It is the cross.

The cross fulfills and confirms the self-emptying tradition of every religion. The atonement is life in death. It is also glory in humiliation. It is exaltation in lowliness. It is wealth in poverty. It is freedom in obedience. The skies darkened, yet light showed forth. He was utterly alone, yet was the way back to full companionship and community in communion. He was abandoned, yet never alone. On the cross, he renounced all to save everything. He totally emptied himself—even of himself—in order to fulfill himself.

The cross is the single most exalted symbol of the Catholic Christian faith. There are other symbols, such as the dove and the flame—both of which represent the Holy Spirit. But none of them is as complete as the cross.

This simple symbol is meant to draw all people to Jesus, yet it sometimes has repulsed them. This repulsion is sometimes not their fault. It is rather often the fault of those who use the cross as a weapon.

For example, the Roman emperor Constantine saw a cross in the sky and heard a voice telling him to go and conquer with this sign. Since then, the cross has been seen on the shields and banners of violent battle. This may have had noble and sincere beginnings, but it ended in countless wars being fought, violence being unleashed, and precious human life being indiscriminately slaughtered—all in the name of Jesus, the Prince of Peace.

Likewise, the cross became a symbol of religious intolerance during the Spanish Inquisition. This ideological holy war went far past the directions Rome had given for establishing doctrinal purity among the faithful. How many helpless and simple innocents were tortured to obtain confessions of heresy they neither espoused nor understood, only to be "mercifully" killed before being thrown onto the flames. Protestants, also, have resorted to torture and cruel death to "convert" Catholics to their cause, and have engaged in their own share of bloody and senseless wars in Jesus' name.

By our hypocrisy and error, the cross has on occasion come to symbolize the exact opposite of what it originally meant. As a result, many people have an immediate, almost subconscious reaction against it. Instead, the cross should remind all people of what it truly means to be fully human and alive in God's world.

## SOUL SACRIFICE

THE SALVATION JESUS brings us takes us beyond theology and logic to love mystery. It impacts body and soul but goes beyond them to the realm of pure spirit. It includes knowledge of God, but it transcends human knowledge, bringing a new mystical enlightenment to all and everything. It is knowing in unknowing, clarity in cloud.

This takes us beyond logic to mystery. Mystery is the language of love, yet it goes beyond either thought or emotion to pure intuition. It includes the body and the soul but goes beyond them to the realm of pure spirit. It includes knowable human energies, yet it goes beyond to the realm of pure human essence, beyond all description or knowledge, bringing a new mystical definition and knowledge to all and everything. It is knowing in unknowing, clarity in cloud, pure and deep memory by sitting and forgetting. It is God's light in divine darkness, God's Word in awesome silence, God's pure action in overwhelming and deep stillness.

This breaks through beyond apparent realities to Reality. It goes beyond superficial understandings of the mind, even regarding religion, to eternal and infinite Mind, from time and space to Eternity and Infinity. It renounces all external perceptions and understandings that have been used by God to bring it truly to this point of growth and development, in order to break through to the ultimate interior perception and understanding in intuition and spirit. This awareness is the rebirth of the spirit, the essence of the child within. Once reborn, the essential spirit brings new life and perception to the energies of soul and body—to thoughts, emotions, and actions—and to all our perceptions of people, living creatures, and things. It even brings a rebirth to our perception of God—of Father, Son, and Holy Spirit.

It is a complete rebirth, a whole new way of living and perceiving all and everything. It is as if we had been living and perceiving with closed eyes. Now our eyes have been opened. Everything and everyone has been made new. We have been made new. We have been reborn, born again in the cross of Jesus.

In a sense, this is much like chewing one of those pieces of gum that has a solid shell with a liquid center. The outside is good. It is even necessary to hold it all together. But once you "break through" to the center, the outside is enlivened with a whole new sweetness and freshness. The outer supports the inner. The inner is "beyond" the outer. But once the inner is discovered, it permeates all that came before.

In theological and anthropological terms, the body and soul house and protect the spirit. But once you build on and go beyond body and soul and break through to spirit, the spirit enlivens all that came before. One's whole being is totally reborn.

This is what all religions seek in one way or another. Some call it Samadhi, or Satori, or Kensho. Others call it spiritual alchemy, or refining the spirit through energy and vitality. But Jesus brings this experience on in a unique and extraordinary way. He is the way, the truth, and the life. He is awakening for Buddhists and Hindus, the way for Taoists and Confucianists. He joins them all in a common ground and fulfills them all.

## THE END OF THE STORY

THE STORY of the real Jesus doesn't end there; instead, it extends into eternity, beyond the end of time itself.

The first Christians didn't fully understand the depths of this mystery of the atonement. Most were convinced they were living through the culmination of human history. They believed Jesus was coming back very soon to take them to heaven, so they didn't have much of a long-term view of living the Christian life.

But Jesus didn't return to whisk them away to paradise, and these disciples of Jesus began to realize that God's timing is not always our timing. "Soon" for God may be millennia for humanity.

Suddenly, Christians began to talk about issues like spiritual maturity and deepening in the understanding of their faith. They grew in wisdom. They grew in mystery. Soon sages, holy people, and mystics appeared and began to teach believers about going deeper into the things of God. The discipline of Christian contemplation was widely taught, leading to the development of monasticism as a way of life for hermits and mystics, clerical, and laypeople alike.

In the process, Christians discovered such practices were close to the real way of Jesus Christ himself. He was no longer a figure "out there" to be followed. He was right there within them, Spirit in spirit, so that the two now became one.

Again, it is Saint Paul in whom we can most clearly see this progression. In the beginning, he writes extensively of the Second Coming and is very enthusiastic about the return of Jesus. The cross, however, is only a way to resurrection and forgiveness, but his theology of the cross retains a strong dualism. Paul sees a sharp dichotomy between eternity and this present reality.

As Paul grows older, his emphasis shifts to the cross and the mystery of love union. Where once he looked externally to the imminent Second Coming of Christ, he now begins to mellow and mature, looking more and more to the gift of the Spirit within. Now he writes, "I live, no longer I, but Christ lives in me" (GALATIANS 2:20). By the end of his earthly life, Paul was seeing less of a distinction between the coming of Christ to earth at the end of time and his own daily, ongoing mystical experience of the risen Christ.

Just as Jewish blood sacrifices prepared the way for Jesus, doctrine prepares the way for faith and experience, or that which Saint Bonaventure calls "perfect enlightening of the mind." As he says:

> Since, therefore, an image is an expressed likeness, when our mind contemplates, in Christ the Son of God, our own humanity so wonderfully exalted is so ineffably present in him; and when we thus behold in one and the same being both the first and the last, the highest and the lowest, the circumference and the center, the alpha and the omega, the caused and the cause, the creator and the created creature . . . then our mind reaches a perfect object . . . it reaches with God the perfection of enlightenment.

Devote yourself to the teaching of the apostles, the Church fathers, and others who tell us about the real Jesus, as well as the doctrines of faith and morality. Build upon these things and follow them to the mystical union to which they all point. There is a strong mystical and contemplative heritage in Catholic Christianity. Both are from God, and both are strong traditions in the Church.

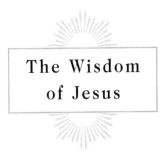

# The Wisdom of Jesus

IT'S MUSIC—NOT WRITING OR SPEAKING—THAT IS MY PRImary gift from God. My music can often express far more than my written or spoken words ever can, and through the years I have seen how one song well sung can touch people far more deeply than a library of books or a month of Sunday sermons.

Still, even the most beautiful songs in the world pale in comparison to the words spoken centuries ago by the man who was the greatest teacher who ever lived. Jesus and the wise words he spoke echo down through the ages. They remain as powerful and as relevant today as they were two thousand years ago.

The wisdom of Jesus is much different from the babel of words, advertising messages, and news reports that bombard us today. We live in an information age, and most of the messages we hear are designed to deliver facts and fantasies to our busy minds.

The words of Jesus have a deeper purpose. In addition to giving us information about God and about how we should live our lives, Jesus' words can bring powerful supernatural transformation. And the two major communication tools Jesus used when he spoke were parables and paradoxes.

Parables—those brief, simple stories—are designed to illustrate important points. The New Testament Gospels of Luke, Matthew, and Mark record nearly sixty of Jesus' parables and parabolic statements. In the parable of the prodigal son (LUKE 15:11–32), Jesus creates a story about a young man who leaves his family and wastes his life and money to show us what can happen when people turn their back on God and his love. And in the parable of the sower (MARK 4:3–20), Jesus uses the clear and straightforward language of farming ("A sower went out to sow") to illustrate that just as some kinds of soil are more fertile than others, so some human hearts are more receptive to God than others are.

Paradoxes are statements that are—or at least appear to be— self-contradictory or mutually exclusive. For example, when Jesus says, "Blessed are the poor in spirit, for theirs is the kingdom of heaven," he is teaching that wealth can be found through poverty. As we will see, Jesus used paradoxes to help his listeners see beyond the facts of everyday experience to the deeper truths that often lie hidden under the surface of things.

Studying the parables and paradoxes of Jesus, we can begin to receive the wisdom he has to offer us, and our lives can be transformed in the process.

## UNLOCKING THE MYSTERIES OF GOD

ONE OF JESUS' best-known parables comes from Luke 15:4–7:

> What man among you having a hundred sheep and losing one
> of them would not leave the ninety-nine in the desert and go after

*the lost one until he finds it? And when he does find it, he sets it on his shoulders with great joy and, upon his arrival home, he calls together his neighbors and says to them, "Rejoice with me because I have found my lost sheep." I tell you, in just the same way there will be more joy in heaven over one sinner who repents than over ninety-nine righteous people who have no need of repentance.*

I once sat and watched an Israeli shepherd near a cave hermitage located below Shepherd's Field, which is outside of Bethlehem. For much of the day, he patiently sat and watched his flock. He seemed calm and unhurried, but was able to respond at a second's notice to any danger to his flock. I watched in amazement as he moved quietly, surely, and gently among the sheep, touching each one in the course of the day. He knew his sheep.

Watching this shepherd, I was struck by the power of Jesus' parable. The way the shepherd cared for his sheep gave me a new understanding of how passionately God loves us. And that's how parables are designed to work.

Jesus teaches not only by quoting scripture, which he could do with mastery, but by quoting nature and the common experiences of humanity. In fact, Jesus actually quoted creation more than he quoted scripture, even though the doctrines found in the Bible had a preeminent place in his message. Jesus was able to see the lessons of God in both the Biblical revelation and the natural world, and his parables conveyed amazing depth with surprising simplicity.

Jesus didn't invent parables or analogies, which had long been an important part of the Middle Eastern and East Asian wisdom traditions, but the church fathers and monastic fathers employed these literary devices, using them to convey things both plain and mysterious at the same time. Being both simple and mystical, parables are childlike without becoming either childish or overly sophisticated. They break through to the spirit, communicating a truth both knowable to the mind and emotions and unknowable except by the intuition of the spirit. Once they break through, they permeate all with new and deeper meanings that both fulfill and confound the old. This is the power of the parable. It is the language of the mystic and the saint. And it was the preferred teaching tool of Jesus.

As we rediscover the real Jesus—the Middle Eastern Jewish Jesus—let us look seriously to his parables. Jesus' parables speak of his simplicity. They speak of his wisdom. They speak of his mystery that is yet accessible to all. They speak with words the truth beyond all telling, the truth of Jesus, the only begotten Son of God.

Parables point us toward a truth without trying to define it fully. In the hands of Jesus, the truth "is like" this or that experience from daily life or from creation. He does not just come right out and deliver a message in a propositional, purely rational manner. Instead, he points toward the objective or knowable aspect of that truth, without violating its mystery through overdefinition.

Straightforward propositional communication—which is precisely the kind that bombards us every day—leaves little room for mystery. It proclaims, "This is the truth," reducing the mystery and wonder of Truth to concrete theological or philosophical statements. Parables, on the other hand, clearly point to the truth, but without violating the mystery of Truth. This allows each of us to experience the truth of Jesus' words in a manner that's personally meaningful and transformative.

Parables are very simple. They communicate to children as well as to scholars. And there was always something about children that Jesus loved. Once, when a group of children was brought to Jesus, he said, "the kingdom of heaven belongs to such as these." This wasn't an endorsement of childishness. Rather, Jesus was reminding all of us to honor the joy and awesome wonder of creation and creation's God. Likewise, Jesus' parables are childlike without being childish.

In a sense, those who tell parables must be children, scholars, and mystics all at once. They must know simplicity, complexity, and mystery as a personal experience before they possess the personal authority to tell parables in a way that will reach their hearers at every level. They may say the words, but without this living authority, the parables will fall flat, not reaching anyone's heart, mind, or spirit.

The teacher of parables must also be conversant with creation and with human nature, as well as with scripture. The parables of Jesus, such as the parable of the lost sheep, contain profound insights about the natural world, human nature, and the ways of God.

But the parables of Jesus were designed to do much more than provide intellectual insight. They were designed to help us unlock the mysteries of God and experience the life-changing transformation God can bring.

## JESUS AS THE BRIDGE
## BETWEEN EAST AND WEST

JESUS WAS A Middle Eastern Jew whose life and teachings spawned the Western world's dominant faith. But his message truly transcends all distinctions of East and West, and his living legacy represents a crucial cultural bridge between the East and all of Western civilization. In the same way, the writings of the early Church fathers demonstrate their mastery of parable, paradox, and mystery, and this mastery helped them communicate the Christian message to people both Eastern and Western.

In the succeeding centuries, however, much of the Christian Church has become more and more Westernized. As a result, we have lost important parts of the Eastern Catholic experience. As our world becomes more of a global village, with the advent of mass communication and transportation, many Westerners are encountering the importance, relevance, and majesty of the East again. Pope John Paul II has repeatedly encouraged the body of Christ to learn once again how to "breathe with both lungs," East and West, rather than only from the one Western lung, as much of Christianity has been doing for too long. If we can begin to understand how wonderfully Jesus incorporated the Eastern wisdom tradition into his teaching, we will be better prepared to express the Christian faith with "both lungs," as the Pope has asked us to do.

Jesus used parables, but they can also be found in the Old Testament, and in Jewish rabbinical writings, as well as faiths we traditionally think of as Eastern. The Buddha used parables and analogies at length. The Koran is filled with parables. In short, the parable was a very important communication tool which was used by many Middle Eastern religious teachers and wise men.

As we have said before, Jesus was a Jew. Jews were a Middle Eastern people. And Christianity was also largely Middle Eastern in its earliest forms. To understand either the Jews or the early Christians, we must have at least some appreciation for the Eastern environment in which they appeared. Otherwise, we can miss the true flavor of the very faith we profess.

Today, most people think of Christianity as a Western religion. In earlier chapters we have discussed how Saint Paul successfully spread the Gospel west in his missionary journeys, globalizing it by taking it to much of the Roman Empire and articulating its creeds in the language of the Greek philosophers.

Of course, Christianity was not the only Middle Eastern faith to follow such a course. Jews had been "Hellenized" centuries before. Muslims also began to integrate aspects of Western philosophy and mysticism into Islam's language and style in the centuries after the death of Mohammed.

But Christians were wildly successful in their efforts to Westernize their faith. Unfortunately, what was gained through these efforts of Western missionary expansion resulted in Christianity's losing much of its original Eastern orientation. Though apostles such as Saint Thomas took the Gospel as far East as India, most written accounts of the early Church were produced by Westerners, giving the faith a more Western slant.

But parables are a way in which we can return to the Eastern Jesus. Both East and West seek a Universal, an Absolute Truth, amid the particulars and relative truths of life. Both seek a reference point, an anchor in the storm. The West does this more by logic and mental speculation. The East does it by mystical experience and the breakthrough to the soul and spirit. Both include logic and mystery, but the tone of the West is toward the former, and the tone of the East is toward the latter.

By studying the wisdom of Jesus, we can begin to recapture many of Christianity's important Eastern accents. Where once Christians used Western philosophies to bring a more Eastern Jesus to the West, so now we can use the Eastern religions and philosophies of our day to bring a Western Christianity back to the East, and in so doing, rediscover the real Jesus once again.

Recently, the 1998 Synod of the Catholic Bishops of Asia called for a greater sensitivity to Eastern culture and religion, and cited past Western insensitivity as a primary reason why Christianity has failed to spread throughout the East, even in India, which according to tradition was visited by Saint Thomas, one of the early Church's twelve apostles who is also known by his Greek name, Didymus. According to the apocryphal New Testament book, the Acts of Thomas, Thomas was an extreme ascetic who traveled to India on a missionary journey and was martyred there.

Some Western bishops have responded with fear that greater sensitivity to or dialogue with the East will compromise

Christianity's unique character. They caution that the Church may lose its absolute truth in faith and morality through too much integration with a system more comfortable with a more relative approach to objective truth. While such cautions are valid and worth noting, a simple return to the original Jesus might solve the whole problem without compromising any major Christian belief. This will satisfy both East and West without violating either.

One of the ways Westerners can do this is by studying the parables of Jesus. Parables are helpful tools that use simple words and ideas to help us break through to the spirit. They speak of truths that are knowable to the mind and emotions but can only be experienced by the intuition of the spirit.

## A WISDOM BEYOND WORDS

LIKE OTHER EASTERN TEACHERS, Jesus made frequent use of paradox, a technique of ancient wisdom traditions that involves the use of contradictions to break through beyond the seeming duality of opposites to a deeper truth of union and oneness. A paradox is a seeming contradiction that speaks a deeper mystery of truth.

Jesus' life and ministry were marked by paradox. Both the incarnation (God becoming humanity and living among us) and the cross (Christ's death by crucifixion to give us all eternal life) are supreme paradoxes. And in his teaching ministry, Jesus used words to speak of wordless truths. Through paradox, Jesus took us from mere external and objective truth to wisdom, the greatest gift of knowledge.

Probably the greatest example of this paradoxical wisdom of Jesus is found in the Beatitudes (MATTHEW 5:3–12). These powerful statements—each of which begins with the words, "Blessed are"—form the beginning of the Sermon on the Mount, which is probably Jesus' best-known and most-loved address.

The sermon begins with Jesus going up a mountain and being seated. This is a symbol that Jesus speaks from the authority of having already climbed these spiritual steps himself. And interestingly, the image of Jesus teaching from a mount, or high place, connects his teaching to the Eastern wisdom traditions that often featured a disciple or student sitting at the feet of a master, or guru, on a mountaintop.

One can also see the Sermon on the Mount, which is a centerpiece of the New Testament, as a parallel to Moses receiving the Ten Commandments, which is a centerpiece of the Old Testament. Thus, just as the Law of God was a focus of the Old Testament, so these Beatitudes are a focus of the New Testament. But unlike the Commandments, which were regulations written on stone by the finger of God, the new covenant Jesus announces springs from his own living authority as the Incarnate Word. He first lived it before he taught it. He had to "take its seat." He now invites all to come and be seated with him in the living authority of a whole new way of life. The Buddhists say students must sit in the Buddha's seat. Likewise, Christians must now sit at the feet of Christ.

Jesus begins his sermon with a series of paradoxes: the wealth of God's kingdom can be found in poverty; consolation and joy can be experienced in sorrow and mourning; power and privilege can be had by embracing meekness and lowliness; being filled happens by embracing the emptiness of hunger and thirst for holiness; and a triumphal reign is achieved by embracing persecution and rejection. Jesus also speaks of the classical wisdom themes of showing mercy and being single-hearted, or pure of heart, in order to find the way of God.

These powerful, paradoxical Beatitudes are merely the prelude for all that follows in the Sermon on the Mount. They introduce us to a whole new way of perceiving reality, a whole new way of thinking. They are a logic beyond the logic of old. They go beyond the superficial and the obvious to the interior and the subtle, beyond flesh to soul and spirit, beyond space and time to the infinite and the eternal. They go beyond opposites to oneness through the door of mystery and paradox.

But far from being mere esoteric wordplay for the sophisticated few, the Beatitudes penetrate to the heart and soul of the poor and the simple, as well as to the educated and the learned. They are for all: rich and poor, simple and wise. They are universal, catholic, and full. As Jesus himself is the door to the sheepfold—the way, the truth, and the life—these words are gateways to the mysteries of God. No one can come to the intimacies and mysteries of God except through these. There is no other way.

## LESSONS FOR THE JOURNEY

FOLLOWING THIS SIMPLE yet lofty beginning, Jesus delivers a teaching from which we can glean six important lessons about the spiritual life. Each of these lessons illustrates a key idea of the Christian faith, and each reveals Jesus' unique place within the tradition of Eastern wisdom teachers. Let us look at and learn from these lessons:

*Keep the faith* (MATTHEW 5:10–16)

Jesus encourages his disciples to keep going and not fall back from completing the course. Other masters do the same. I am reminded of the Zen Buddhist roshi who encourages his monks to make extraordinary efforts in their lifestyle and meditation practice to prepare for their long seshin (which is an intense one-week period of reflection that is in some ways similar to the Christian's Lent or the Muslim's Ramadan).

No matter the religious tradition, many disciples mistake initial insight or zeal for the deeper awakening that awaits those who make the longer journey requiring greater—and steadier—zeal. After these initial awakenings to wisdom through paradox and mystery, Jesus encourages his disciples to keep going, not to let their "salt lose its taste," and not to let their light to be covered up.

### Truth matters (MATTHEW 5:17–20)

Jesus cautions his disciples against throwing out all of God's objective truths. Even though he is taking them beyond mere fact to the realm of awakening to paradox and mystery, he clearly states that all the precepts of the old Law are to be fulfilled, and with an even greater zeal now that a new interior motivation is a reality in their lives.

A similar message can be found in other religions. Especially as Eastern religions came west to Europe and America, there was a tendency to discard all the objective precepts. One can see this very clearly in the case of Buddhism, especially among many Western disciples who have embraced Zen. The masters who survived this period (and many didn't!) all cautioned against this tendency toward discarding fundamental truths. The mystical awakenings and the illogical antics of schools like Zen must always be placed squarely in their context of a Hinduism and Buddhism that have clear and exacting moral and ascetic precepts and practices.

As Jesus tells us, the same is true for Christians. To circumvent the basic disciplines is to rob oneself of the greater mystical treasures that await those who are humble and obedient enough to submit completely to a master and follow the way.

### Morality matters (MATTHEW 5:21–37)

Jesus also states loudly and clearly right from the beginning that following him into the realm of rebirth of the original child of God, through logic to paradox and mystery, does not free anyone to live an unlawful, immoral, or blasphemous life. Just as the breakthrough to mystery does not free one from the godly reality of objective truth and logic, neither does spiritual liberation free one from the responsibility to lead a disciplined, moral life.

*We can experience rebirth* (JOHN 3:3–8)

Moving to the core of the sermon, Jesus explains how we can break free from the prison of sinful thoughts, emotions, words, and action to the freedom of purity and rebirth through an interior transformation, a change of soul and spirit. He has already shown us the way through the paradox and mystery of the Beatitudes. Now he shows us the result: freedom from the anger and lust that cause broken relationships, destroying marriages and leading to divorce.

He shows us a whole new way of speaking, one that is gentle, honest, peaceful, and true. He also reveals a whole new way of facing and resolving conflict through a nonresistant heart, peaceful and detached, filled with love and compassion. The spiritual rebirth Jesus proclaims brings freedom from the interior judgments that so plague not only our own thoughts and emotions but every relationship they affect.

*True religion* (MATTHEW 6:1–18)

Jesus also speaks about true religion and prayer. Prayer is to be more a matter of intentions and spirit of real faith and belief, and less a matter of external words that thinly cover our doubt. Fasting and almsgiving become more a matter of pure intention than of the subtle religious self-righteousness that usually seeks to be noticed.

*Fleeing the cares of the world* (MATTHEW 6:19–34)

Last, Jesus speaks of a renunciation and detachment from external possessions that is the classical way to interior freedom in every major religion of the world. Jesus and Christianity are no exception. In fact, Jesus demands it of every disciple, not just of a few.

The logic goes like this: Possessing things, people, or ideas gives rise to unruly passions, especially when these possessions are denied. Unruly passions corrupt both thoughts and actions, and imprison both in a habitual pattern of life that is illusory and false. Such false and illusory habit patterns of thought, emotion, and action keep us from breaking through to the deeper realm of the spirit and reordering our whole life around the love, joy, and peace that are its natural abode.

In short, Jesus calls us all to an external poverty that breeds an internal poverty of spirit, a way of detachment and peace that frees us up to live lives of real compassion and love. Thus we are brought to the very first Beatitude about finding wealth in poverty. The whole Sermon on the Mount revolves around this theme, and in the Beatitudes Jesus' message breaks through to the paradox and mystery that bring enlightenment and rebirth to one's entire life.

## THE REAL MESSAGE
## OF THE REAL JESUS

JESUS TEACHES US through words that point beyond mere logic of truth to the mystery of love. Love and logic combine to bring forth divine wisdom. The knowable and the unknowable are united in a wisdom known best beyond the emotions or the mind in pure spiritual intuition.

These lessons of Jesus are road signs to the experience of rebirth and enlightenment that illuminates all other experience and knowledge. Stay on the surface, and true though it is, this wisdom has only a beginner's effect. Move deeper into thought, emotion, words, and action, and you begin to make progress. Go to the deepest center and break through the seeming opposites to the mystical oneness of intuition and spirit, and you find the perfection spoken of in the Sermon on the Mount by Jesus.

Let us hear the words of wisdom completely: body, soul, and spirit, with logic, love, and contemplative intuition, and so break through to a wisdom beyond telling or silence, knowing or unknowing, logic or mystery.

This wisdom of the real Jesus.

# The Mother of God

MELODY IS AN IMPORTANT PART OF EVERY SONG, BUT HAR-mony adds depth and beauty to music, producing a creative tension while serving to accentuate the melody in new and exciting ways.

God wants us to experience his mystical music in our lives, and one of the ways we do this is by working in harmony with God. Mary was a unique and important person who cooperated with the divine plan in a magnificent way. She offers us much we can learn about working in harmony with God. If Jesus is God's melody, Mary is a beautiful harmony.

Through the Incarnation, God took on human form in Jesus. Thus the Incarnation strikes a perfect balance and harmony between the divine and the human. God was the initiator, but humanity's role as cooperator with God was of extraordinary importance. We see this cooperation gracefully and beautifully expressed in Mary, the young woman who cooperated with God to bring forth Jesus, who the ancient creeds of the faith declare was "true God and true Man."

Gnostics—both ancient and modern—have a real problem with this. They believe the Fall means that all flesh and physical reality is evil. This view was a reflection of a philosophical dualism that has plagued religion of all kinds since the beginning. According to this view, the physical world is flawed and bad, and the spiritual world is transcendent and good. As a result, Gnostic forms of Christianity have historically lacked the full balance and harmony of true Christianity.

The Gnostic view—which remains popular today through a number of books called Gnostic "gospels"—has no comprehension of how Jesus, the son of God, is Incarnated, "taking on flesh" to become fully human yet remaining fully divine. Rather, Gnostics view the earthly Jesus as merely some kind of materialized ghost or spirit. And if Jesus was not physically born, there is no need for Mary, for the Incarnation was not really real but was illusory at best.

But the ancient and historic faith of Christianity that has been handed down through the centuries affirms the Incarnation, and venerates Mary as our Co-redemptress with Christ and the Co-mediatrix of God's grace. The following pages will tell us much about this amazing woman, and why she is a model of godliness for us all.

## MIRACLE IN A MANGER

Two thousand years ago in a humble stable in Bethlehem of Judea, Mary gave birth to Jesus, who was both divine and human. In the Christian tradition, this miracle is known as the virgin birth. Frequently the Gospel refers to Jesus as the Son of God or the Son of Man. In addition, the ancient creeds of the faith call Jesus "Son of God, Son of Mary." And in A.D. 431, Church leaders meeting at the Council of Ephesus conferred on her the title Theotokus, or the "bearer" or "Mother of God."

Anyone who has ever attended a Christmas Eve church service has heard at least portions of the Gospel of Luke's story of Mary, who through the mysterious work of the Holy Spirit and a miracle that was heralded by the angel Gabriel conceived a child who would be named Jesus.

Even though Mary was to be married to a man named Joseph, the two had not engaged in sexual relations. She questioned the angel, "How can this be, since I have no relations with a man?" But thankfully, even though Mary did not completely understand, she cooperated with the Spirit.

The Bible records her wholehearted compliance with the work of God: "Behold, I am the handmaid of the Lord. May it be done to me according to your word" (LUKE 1:38). There were no more questions. No doubt. No human rationalization. Her response was pure surrender and humility, absolute "yes" to the will of God in her life.

There is a passage in Luke called "the Canticle of Mary," or "the Magnificat" (LUKE 1:46–55), which features Mary's spontaneous outburst of joy at being chosen to be God's special vessel. I have adapted her speech in my song, "Holy Is His Name":

*My soul proclaims the greatness of the Lord;*
*my spirit exalts in God my savior.*
*For he has looked with mercy on my lowliness,*
*and my name will forever be exalted.*
*For the mighty God has done great things for me,*
*and his mercy will reach from age to age.*
*And holy, holy, holy is his name.*

Today, millions of Catholic Christians around the world still honor Mary, who is seen as a great heroine of the faith for her willingness to work in harmony with God in this wonderful event. There is also a growing appreciation of Mary among evangelical Christians, many of whom find valuable lessons in Mary's example, both for the individual believer and the whole Church. I have also heard numerous reports of Pentecostal believers who practice such "Catholic" devotions as praying the rosary as a means of growing closer to Jesus. Mary is even honored by non-Christian believers as well, and is mentioned nearly three dozen times in the Koran.

The purpose of all this adulation is not to focus on Mary alone, but rather to illustrate the fact that if we will dare have faith as Mary did, Jesus can be born into our lives today, in the midst of the here and the now.

Not all of us will be summoned by the angel Gabriel, but to each and every one of us, God announces a portion of his will, his plan for us to help bring salvation to the world. God can do this through the inner promptings of the Holy Spirit deep within spirit and soul, as well as through the ordinary circumstances of life. God can also announce his will to us through the teaching authority of spiritual fathers and mothers within the Church, including abbots, abbesses, and elders within monastic communities, and personal spiritual directors for lay believers. Most important, God guides us through the magisterium—or teaching authority—of the Church itself. All of these many and varied ways, when rightly discerned, can reveal and announce God's plan to us.

We may question, as Mary did. But somewhere deep beneath the questions is the gift of faith implanted within us in the beginning by God. If we look deeply to find that gift of faith, we will also say our yes to God. We will find peace, and all our questions and doubts can be still. Then the greatest potential of human life will become a reality: Jesus will be born into our lives, and through our lives into the world. Then, with Saint Paul, we can say, "I have been crucified with Christ; yet I live, no longer I, but Christ lives in me" (GALATIANS 2:19–20).

It's important to remember that Jesus is the subject Mary points us to, Mary does not point us to herself. Mary is important because Jesus is more important. Mary is honored and venerated because Jesus, her Son, is to be worshiped and adored as God. Mariology, which is the study and devotion to Mary, exists only to enrich and protect Christology, not to take away the emphasis from Christ.

Ultimately, Mary forces us all to confront these questions: Can we be the "bearer" of God? Can we be the "mother" of God? Can we bring God to the Church, humanity, and all creation by giving birth to the real Jesus right here in our time?

The example of Mary gives an affirmative answer to all of these questions, and reminds us that we are all to continue this maternal ministry of continually birthing Jesus into our world.

## THREE-PART HARMONY

THROUGH THE CENTURIES, Church leaders, theologians, and saints have struggled with precisely how to explain Mary and her unique role in God's mystical music of salvation.

The way Mary yielded, working in harmony with the will of God, is central. In addition, there are three important aspects of Mary's cooperation with God. These are the Immaculate Conception, the Assumption into heaven, and Mary's status as "Ever Virgin."

The ancient Church fathers spent much time vigorously debating these Marian traditions. And interestingly, neither Saint Bonaventure nor Saint Thomas Aquinas ultimately believed, for example, in Mary's Immaculate Conception—a complex concept that was not articulated with precision until the Franciscan thinker John Duns Scotus did so in the fifteenth century. Each of these three concepts teach us much about how we can work in harmony with God.

## WITHOUT SIN

ACCORDING TO THE DOCTRINE of the Immaculate Conception, the Church teaches, Mary was kept from original sin in order to give birth to Jesus.

The reasoning goes that Jesus had to be sinless in order to die on a cross and bear humanity's sins. But if he inherited original sin by being born of one who had original sin, he himself would inherit the "wages," or effects, of original sin, which are death.

How, then, could Mary, who was born before Christ died to save the world from sin, be kept from sin herself? The answer is through the cross of her Son, Jesus. Though Jesus' death on the cross happened in time and space, its effects extend throughout all time and all the cosmos. Think of the cross as a wonderful and miraculous spiritual time warp with the power to break the cycle of suffering and spiritual darkness throughout eternity.

Just as the ancients of the Old Testament and people not yet born will be saved by faith through the cross of Christ, so Mary was kept free from original sin beginning with the moment of her own conception—her Immaculate Conception—by the work of her Son on the cross. Mary's Immaculate Conception is the passageway enabling humanity to approach the door of salvation and find freedom from humanity's endless cycle of sin, suffering, and death. Jesus is that doorway, but it was Mary's working in harmony with God that made the doorway possible.

Mary is not to be worshiped, but she is to be venerated. As Augustine once said in one of his homilies, worship is given to God alone, but veneration is given to angels and saints. And certainly Mary is our foremost saint.

She is not God, but she is the bearer of God. Catholics consider her to have been kept from all sin, but she is not all-knowing, even of God's plans. Many times throughout her life she questioned God: when a youthful Jesus left her and Joseph to "be about my father's business" in the Temple; when Jesus performed his first miracle, turning water into wine at the wedding feast in Cana; and when she interrupted one of his teaching sessions. Most important, she questioned the angel Gabriel when he announced the upcoming birth of Christ to her (much as Zechariah questioned Gabriel concerning the birth of John the Baptist). In all of this, she is far from omniscient. She fails to grasp God's plan. She is quite human indeed!

Perhaps the loudest proclamation of Mary's immaculate behavior is her own silence, as well as the silence of Scripture about Mary. Nowhere do we read of her butting in where she was not supposed to be. She never crowed, "That's my son." She never claimed special privileges or rights. Rather, she is always present, standing silent and faithful.

It was Mary's humble faithfulness that led the early Church to recognize this immaculate jewel that had stood so silently in their midst, and to heap titles and honors upon her. While Peter was appointed the early believers' leader, no one—including Peter, the bishops, and the popes—has ever been given a sanctity equaling hers. She is always ranked first among the saints.

Saints who have followed Mary's way of lowliness and service, such as Mother Teresa of Calcutta, have also been given more honor than was accorded to official Church leaders who were their contemporaries. Paradoxically, the call to lowliness and humility is a higher call. It is a call to complete self-surrender and emptiness, to servanthood without special recognition or position, to silence and lowliness.

This lowly harmony with the will of God is the highest and most immaculate call of all. It conveys an authority beyond ordination or special position and recognition. This is the lesson of Mary's Immaculate Conception.

## FALLING ASLEEP

MARY GIVES US a tantalizing glimpse of heaven: a destination that is real, but beyond the reality we presently know. Its streets will be "like transparent gold," and our new bodies will be like Jesus' resurrected body. As we have seen, there was a brief period after Jesus rose from the dead but before he ascended into heaven, and during this time his body was a dramatic display of the mysteries and paradoxes of time and eternity, body and spirit. At some times, Jesus was recognizable, but at other times, disciples who had been with him for years did not know it was him. Also, he was able to eat, and his body still bore the scars of his crucifixion on the cross, yet he could simply appear at will within a room or vanish from sight into thin air.

The Assumption—the teaching that Mary was taken immediately into heaven at the end of her earthly life without tasting the fullness of death—is a natural outgrowth of her Immaculate Conception.

Over the centuries, there has been much debate about precisely how the Assumption was accomplished, but one thing is clear: Mary's body was never found. Her tomb, like that of her Son, was always seen as empty by the early Church. Though there's a tomb that tradition ascribes to Mary, from the beginning it has been understood to be empty. There is not one contemporary account of her body remaining in a tomb.

Looking at the broad span of Biblical history, many see the Assumption as a type, or symbol, of the eternal life that is promised to all who trust God. In the Old Testament, Elijah was assumed into heaven right before Elisha's eyes. And earlier, Enoch, a righteous man the Bible describes as one who "walked with God," was also taken to heaven without tasting death: "He was no longer here, for God took him," say the Scriptures (GENESIS 5:24).

Jesus, who did know bodily death through the crucifixion, also ascended to heaven, his original home. But whereas Jesus was uniquely God's own son, Mary was assumed into heaven as a symbol of the redemption God graciously offers to all humanity. She was a mortal human who shared in the divine by privilege and grace. Her Assumption is one final and absolute proof of the victory of Jesus over sin and death. Or as one saint put it, Mary's assumption represents "our life, our sweetness, and our hope." She "sleeps" to share in his death on the cross, and she is assumed to share in his resurrection and ascension into heaven.

Not all Christians believe in Mary's Assumption, but it is a teaching that contains a greater lesson for us all: that if we follow an immaculate life of humility and purity in Jesus, we will not lose God's promised reward of eternal life in heaven.

Heaven is that place we all long for and desire. It is where our original life as pure children of God will come to pass fully and without hindrance. Mary has already been crowned Queen of Heaven. In time, we also will gain a heavenly crown. In heaven, our child of God will grow to become something beyond what we can possibly expect or imagine. As Paul writes:

*What eye has not seen, and ear has not heard,*
*and what has not entered the human heart,*

*what God has prepared for those who love him,*
*this God has revealed to us through the Spirit*
[1 CORINTHIANS 2:9–10].

Although all of us can try to imagine what heaven is like, it is beyond our present comprehension. Our souls and our bodies are still constrained by space and time, emotions and concepts. Heaven can only be comprehended in spirit by intuition.

God has given us a down payment of this future glory. As one Biblical writer put it, we are "already seated in heavenly places," at the right hand of God the Father. Our spirits are already in eternity and infinity in and through Christ. By intuition in contemplative prayer, or rapture and ecstasy, we are already there. This is mystery and paradox. It is wonder. It is not yet fully manifested. It is "already and not yet."

The Assumption of Mary challenges and encourages all of us to stay faithful to God during this interim period between time and eternity. Mary's Assumption fills us with hope as we "send up our sighs from this valley of suffering and tears."

## PURE OF HEART

THE VIRGIN BIRTH is essential to a full understanding of the perfect harmony and balance of Jesus Christ and his Incarnation. Jesus is both human and divine. His mother is Mary. His father is God, with no human father. If Mary was not a virgin, the divine portion of the balance is jeopardized, and the entire teaching about the uniqueness of Christ collapses like a house of cards. Without the Virgin Birth, Jesus becomes simply another human holy man, prophet, or avatar. Good as that is, it is not the full story of the Incarnation proclaimed by Jesus Christ and the early Christian Church.

Today, there is intense debate in some quarters about the Bible's teaching that Mary was a virgin when she gave birth to Jesus. In addition to teaching the Immaculate Conception and the Assumption, for centuries the Church has proclaimed a third important teaching about Mary: that she remained a virgin even after the birth of Jesus. This "Ever Virgin" teaching is not as crucial as the doctrine of Christ's Virgin Birth, but study makes it clear that the early Church did not believe that Mary and Joseph had any other children.

In the early Church, two separate traditions about Mary developed in the East and the West.

The Eastern tradition holds that Mary had been vowed to perpetual virginity at an early age, and dedicated to God through service and assistance at the Temple. But since it was uncommon for young Jewish girls to remain unmarried into adulthood, an elderly man named Joseph, a widower with older children, agreed to marry Mary, while privately respecting her vow to perpetual virginity.

A more plausible explanation is found in traditions handed down in the Christian West. We still have a treatise written by Saint Jerome, who was responding to a man named Helvidius, who had raised questions about New Testament references to Jesus' "brothers and sisters." Jerome concluded that these people were actually "cousins" born to another biblical Mary, the wife of Clopas. Jerome said the Greek word for cousin is the same as that used for brother and sister, indicating that the supposed siblings were simply close family members. Jerome also indicated that the tradition of Mary as Ever Virgin was commonly embraced by the early church.

These may seem like highly technical discussions, but the point is that the early Church leaders believed Mary was Ever Virgin. They didn't know the specifics of how, but they did accept the teaching as true, and they ardently disagreed with those who questioned or opposed this tradition.

Later commentators say it this way: The Ever Virginity of Mary is not theologically necessary, but it is appropriate. If the Virgin Birth was necessary, then Mary's being Ever Virgin is appropriate. If it was appropriate, it is probable, or likely. In an appropriate way, the Ever Virginity of Mary maintains the beautiful balance and harmony of Mary's role as cooperator in the Incarnation of Christ and a model and mother of the church.

## UNINTENDED CONSEQUENCES

SOME HAVE MISTAKENLY read the Church's teaching on Mary's virginity as a condemnation of sex. This is an unfortunate misunderstanding, even though there is some evidence to support such a notion in the work of some Christian writers. The Church honors the sacredness of the sexual act in the context of marriage. Through the centuries, the Church has been emphatically clear that marriage and sexual union are sacramental, meaning they are visible signs of the invisible grace of God. Only the most extreme ascetics have ever stated that sex was evil, and this view was never accepted by the teaching authority of the Church.

Rather, the lesson our souls can learn from Mary, the Ever Virgin, is that we are called to have virginal hearts, minds, and souls, so that this pure spirit within us all can be set free from the prison of sullied desires and lusts and be reborn in God.

From the time of Moses to the present day, the people God created have shown a propensity for spiritual adultery. We worship idols rather than the living God. Or, as one Bible version puts it, we "go whoring after other gods" (EXODUS 34:15–16). But Mary gives us a model of what it means for Jesus to forgive us of the promiscuous spiritual thoughts, emotions, and actions of our past. She shows us what it means to be transformed from spiritual adultery to being the Brides of Christ.

Mary shows us the way to a life that is virginal and pure, and with God's help, this spiritual purity can be continuous. As in the case of Mary, it can go on forever.

As Mary was, we are betrothed in a spiritual marriage to God. As Mary did, we spiritually give birth to Jesus through a virginal and completely pure conception. As with Mary's, our purity and reverent wonder are maintained by remaining ever-virgin in Christ. Like Mary, we are to be spiritually ever-virgin.

## ROSES IN THE SNOW

THERE IS A FRANCISCAN legend about Mary that perhaps says more to us about the model of Mary than all the hundreds of words that have preceded it.

One day, Brother Giles and some of his companions were walking in the snow-covered mountains of the Assisi area. As they walked, they discussed Mary, debating the meaning of her Immaculate Conception, her Assumption, and her Ever Virginity.

After much intense theological debate that got them nowhere, Brother Giles raised his voice and said, "I believe Mary was conceived without sin. Without sin. Without sin."

Each time Brother Giles said, "Without sin," he struck the snow-covered ground with his staff. On turning around, he and his companions saw to their amazement that a rosebush had appeared in full bloom at each spot where he had struck his staff.

It's often the same with us. Theological debate, though often helpful, takes us only so far. What is needed is action that brings a beautiful rose flower even out of frozen and snow-covered ground.

The flower God wants to bring to brilliant bloom is the fruit of the Holy Spirit. The frozen ground represents our hardened human hearts. Let us begin with our own hearts. If we let God work his miracle in us through Jesus, we will have learned the lessons of Mary. We will have joined with the Mother of God in the everlasting worship of the one true God.

# The Call
# to Discipleship

IN SCRIPTURE, THOSE WHO FOLLOW JESUS IN A SERIOUS WAY
are called disciples. Those who were curious about him and followed him without commitment are called the multitude. Those
who were chosen by Jesus for special leadership among the disciples
were the "apostles," of whom there were twelve.

The word "disciple" is related to the word "discipline." To be a
disciple of Jesus means that we embrace the discipline of his whole
way of life and spirituality. By nature, we may tend toward a different spirituality and lifestyle that is less demanding. As disciples, we
embrace his way, truth, and life as a discipline. It is not always easy.
But it is very rewarding.

Sirach tells us:

*My son, from your youth embrace discipline; thus will you find wisdom with graying hair. As though plowing and sowing, draw close to her; then await her bountiful crops. For in cultivating her you will labor but little and soon you will eat of her fruits. How irksome she is to the unruly! The fool cannot abide her. . . . For discipline is like her name, she is not accessible to many. Listen, my son, and heed my advice; refuse not my counsel. Put your feet into her fetters, and your neck under her yoke. Stoop your shoulders and carry her. . . . Thus will you afterward find rest in her, and she will become your joy. Her fetters will be your throne of majesty* [SIRACH 6:18–30].

How similar this is to the words of Jesus:

*Come to me, all you who labor and are burdened, and I will give you rest. Take my yoke upon you and learn from me, for I am meek and humble of heart; and you will find rest for yourselves. For my yoke is easy, and my burden light* [MATTHEW 11:28–30].

Discipline is a labor of love, God's love for us. The New Testament epistle to the Hebrews quotes the Old Testament book of Proverbs, saying, "God disciplines those he loves." It may not be easy. It may not be fun. But it is for our ultimate good.

Hebrews continues:

*At the time, all discipline seems a cause not for joy but for pain, yet later it brings forth the peaceful fruit of righteousness to those who are trained by it.*

*So strengthen your drooping hands and your weak knees. Make straight paths for your feet, that what is lame may not be dislocated but healed* [HEBREWS 12:11–13].

The road of life has grown crooked and cluttered. God's original path was straight and clear. It takes work, discipline, and God's grace to fix the road. It is so much easier to just leave the road in disrepair. But it is dangerous to us and everyone else who tries to travel upon it. The easy way is dangerous. The way of discipline seems difficult, but it brings peace, justice, and healing.

The burden of life without God's way has grown heavy. We are weary from its weight. To embrace the discipline of the cross of Jesus seems like extra work and weight to the fool, but to the wise, we see it as the way to refreshment and rest. It is the way from darkness to light, from hatred to real love.

It is like exercise. At the time, we often do not feel like exercising, be it the discipline of yoga, tai chi, lifting weights, or running. But if we stay true to the discipline of exercise, we feel much better. We are healthier in mind, body, and spirit. We work better, pray better, and even rest better. Discipline seems as though it will kill us sometimes. It seems to have enslaved us. But a good discipline actually heals us and sets us free.

In the other major religious traditions we have spoken of, there is also a call to discipleship. In classical Hindu yoga, disciples are simply called shishya, meaning "pupil." There are four kinds: the weak, the mediocre, the exceptional, and the extraordinary. The first three are given a particular kind of yoga, such as mantra, or sound; laya, or meditation; and hatha, or force and physical. Only the fourth is to practice all types of yoga. The first kind is unenthusiastic, foolish, fickle, timid, ill, dependent, rude, ill-mannered, and unenergetic. The second is even-minded and patient, desires virtue, uses kind speech, and is moderate. The third is firm in understanding, apt to meditation, self-reliant, liberal-minded, brave, vigorous, faithful, and willing to submit to the guru and yoga practice devotedly and joyfully. The fourth is energetic, enthusiastic, charming, heroic, knowledgeable of scripture, inclined to practice, free from delusion, orderly, youthful, moderate in food and drink, self-controlled, fearless, pure, skillful, generous, a refuge for all people, capable, stable, thoughtful, willing to obey the teacher, patient, good-mannered, observant of the moral and spiritual law, and willing to keep his struggles to himself. He also has kind speech and faith in scripture and is willing to worship God and revere the teacher God works through. He knows vows for his level of practice, and he practices all levels of yoga. This list is exhaustive, but it is enlightening for those who digest it prayerfully.

The student-disciple lives with the teacher. He is called an antevasin, or "one who dwells near." He will be close in order to observe the teacher, and the teacher observes him. He absorbs the spirit of the teacher. Ultimately, the teacher's spirit indwells in him to awaken his dormant spiritual energies.

In classical Hinduism, the law of Manu begins the discipleship of a Brahmin in late childhood/early manhood, at eight to twelve years old. As students of a spiritual teacher, disciples are first initiated by a rite of initiation, upanayana, signifying new birth, after preparation through activities and vows. After that, the student lives with his teacher, submitting totally to a life of renunciation, study of scripture, meditation, prayer, and service in complete obedience and devotion to his teacher. He becomes the teacher's attendant, but he gains much in the exchange. The teacher is given an almost divine place in the student's life, but never more than the student's father and mother, the mother being the most honored.

After many years of discipleship under this monastic type of training, the young Brahmin is considered ready for the three remaining stages of life: marriage and householder (considered the most socially important), forest dweller and hermit (alone or with wife after becoming a grandparent), and sannyasi, total mendicancy in poverty, solitude, and silence (considered the highest stage). The training of the student stage of discipleship is considered foundational to the next three stages of adult life.

Buddhists also practice discipleship, but Tibetan Buddhism in particular emphasizes the role of the guru and the disciple. Most Buddhists pronounce the Three Jewels upon becoming a Buddhist, taking refuge in the Buddha (or enlightenment), the dharma (or teaching), and the sangha (or the community). Tibetan Buddhism adds a fourth jewel, taking refuge in your guru. For Buddhism, in which the Buddha told his disciples that even he could not substitute for their own individual achievement of enlightenment, this might seem unusual. But all Buddhism came out of a tradition where the guru or master/disciple relationship was taken for granted, even if the Buddha tried to correct the abuses of that same relationship that are common to every religion and era.

In the Tibetan Buddhist devotional book *The Supreme Faith: The Rosary of the Precious Gems*, we hear from the beginning, one of the ten causes for regret (the first decade): The holy guru being the guide for the Path, it would be a cause of regret to be separated from him before attaining enlightenment. Or from the Ten Requirements: To carry out the commands of a religious preceptor, one requires confidence and diligence. And: To avoid error in choosing a guru, the disciple requires to tune in to the mind of the spiritual preceptor. Later we are told to "avoid a guru whose heart is set on acquiring worldly fame and possessions." Finally: "Having chosen a religious preceptor, separate yourself from egotism and follow his teachings implicitly." The rest of the rosary is filled with similar injunctions concerning discipleship under a guru. It is very important to Tibetan Buddhism.

Taoism and Confucianism also take for granted the relationship between sage and disciple. Confucianism spread only through the diligent work of Confucius' disciples after his life. The Taoist sage and master in particular emphasizes that book learning of the Tao is not enough. It must be taught through a living truth and way, actually enfleshed in the life of the master. To try to learn the way of the Tao by books alone is destined for failure. As with later Christian monasticism, Confucianists believe that a sincere seeker is given a teacher to match their sincerity. Or as we say, "God provides the right spiritual director for the right seeker."

In all of this is the central concept that spiritual truth is more than just objective concepts. It is a living spiritual reality. It must be learned by life, by living with an older and wiser person who has already walked the way and learned both the successes and the failures of various approaches and methods. The teacher doesn't just teach words. He teaches life, by example, and by word. Furthermore, the master mystically imparts to the disciple not only the spirit of his teaching, but his own personal spin as well. This is mystical. It also can be frightening if you have an inexperienced or false teacher.

Jesus fulfills the role of the master for the disciples in a profound way. The disciples live with Jesus. They hear him preach and teach. They experience his healing and exorcisms of evil. They watch him relate to others, and they relate to him themselves.

They eat with him, sleep in the same camp, travel in the same group. In short, they learn from the Word Incarnate. They are taught by word and example, theory and life. Last, those who stay with him through the Resurrection and Ascension are given his very Spirit at Pentecost. Their discipleship is more than just learning objective truth. It is the reality of sharing mystical mind and Spirit—the mind and Spirit of Jesus himself. It is a matter of continuing incarnation, the Word made flesh through living the way, the truth, and the life of Jesus.

As soon as Jesus begins his public ministry, he calls forth disciples. He calls them by name: Andrew, John, Peter, and Matthew. He even called Judas, who betrayed him. He calls them to "come and see" how he himself lived. In imitation of his example, he calls his disciples to complete renunciation.

He calls every disciple to renounce all to gain everything. He says, "Anyone who follows me must first deny property, wife, children, mother and father, indeed even his very self. He must take up his cross every day and follow in my steps." Again, "Anyone who would be my disciple cannot do so unless he renounce all of his possessions. . . . You cannot serve God and money. You will hate one and love the other, or love one and despise the other."

Here, he gets to the internal reality for such renunciation. It brings total freedom and liberation when embraced properly. As he says in the Sermon on the Mount, "Wherever your treasure is, there will your heart be also." Possessions steal the heart. If we try to possess people or things, we discover that our heart has been enslaved. Renunciation is the way to freedom. Jesus is unafraid to call his disciples to this lifestyle of freedom, a lifestyle he lived himself and exemplified as "the way, the truth, and the life," and "the truth that sets us free."

Jesus himself exemplified this lifestyle of the renunciate, or sannyasi, spoken of by every other major religion. He is the sannyasi of Hinduism, the Buddha and bodhisattva of Buddhism, and the sage of Taoism and Confucianism. He is the Sufi of Islam and the itinerant prophet of the Jews. He fulfills them all perfectly, fully, and uniquely. He affirms this tradition and calls all of his disciples to embrace it without compromise.

The logic of this lifestyle is the same, more or less, in every religion, philosophy, and faith. Desires and passions cloud the mind and pollute the body when left unchecked. This keeps us from breaking through to the spirit and being fully integrated—body, soul, and spirit—as human beings. It keeps us from the right order and priority of spirit, soul, and body as originally designed for us by God as his children.

Renunciation disciplines the body and the thoughts (through meditation and prayer). The thoughts and the bridled body redirect the desires and passions to godly things. Then we break through to spirit in God's Spirit in contemplation. The spirit in God's Spirit then takes us back to God's order and peace by establishing the body as the servant of the soul, and the soul as the servant of the spirit. Then a rebirth in new integration takes place as we are reestablished, born again, as a child of God in God's original plan and purpose of spirit, soul, and body. All is then in harmony. All is then at peace.

Saint Paul speaks of this logic and lifestyle when he says:

> For those who live according to the flesh are concerned with the things of the flesh, but those who live according to the spirit with the things of the spirit. The concern of the flesh is death, but the concern of the spirit is life and peace. . . . For the concern of the flesh is hostility toward God; it does not submit to the law of God, nor can it; and those who are in the flesh cannot please God. But you are not in the flesh; on the contrary, you are in the spirit, if only the Spirit of God dwells in you. Whoever does not have the Spirit of Christ does not belong to him. But if Christ is in you, although the body is dead because of sin, the spirit is alive because of righteousness. If the Spirit of the one who raised Jesus from the dead dwells in you, the one who raised Christ from the dead will give life to your mortal bodies also, through his Spirit that dwells in you. . . . For if you live according to the flesh, you will die, but if by the spirit you put to death the deeds of the body, you will live [ROMANS 8:5–13].

Saint John uses similar words to describe attachment to the fallen and passing world:

> Do not love the world or the things of the world. If anyone loves the world, the love of the Father is not in him. For all that is in the world, sensual lust, enticement for the eyes, and a pretentious life, is not from the Father but is from the world. Yet the world and its enticement are passing away. But whoever does the will of God remains forever [1 JOHN 2:15–17].

At the beginning and conclusion of his famous passage on the fruits of the flesh and the spirit (GALATIANS 5:19–23), Saint Paul says similarly:

> Now the works of the flesh are obvious: immorality, impurity, licentiousness, idolatry, sorcery, hatreds, rivalry, jealousy, outbursts of fury, acts of selfishness, dissensions, factions, occasions of envy, drinking bouts, orgies, and the like. I warned you, as I warned you before, that those who do such things will not inherit the kingdom of God. In contrast, the fruit of the Spirit is love, joy, peace, patience, kindness, generosity, faithfulness, gentleness, self-control. Against such there is no law.

Just to remind ourselves, what are some of these prisons of the flesh? Lewd conduct, impurity, licentiousness (disorderly desire), idolatry, sorcery. But even closer to the home of habits of daily life, he says, hostility, bickering, jealousy, outbursts of rage (anger), selfish rivalries, dissensions (divisions), factions, envy, drunkenness, orgies, and the like. These things, from small nagging habits to major moral disorders, haunt us and imprison us most of our life. Saint Paul says that in this condition, we do the things we hate and don't do the things we want to do, adding that this is imprisonment and death from which the human heart cries to be set free (ROMANS 7).

Then he says, "In contrast, the fruit of the spirit is love, joy, peace, patience, kindness, generosity, mildness, chastity and faith." These are the things the human being has been created for. When they are absent, we seek them.

We find them in Christ by renouncing all and becoming his disciples. If we do not follow him, we will not reach the goal. If we try to avoid discipline or complete renunciation, we cannot really follow. We cannot be disciples. We simply become one of the curious, one of the "multitude," who are spiritually entertained and briefly distracted from the troubles of this fallen world by Jesus, the newest guru, fad, or entertainer in our modern, fast-paced life.

The early Christians lived this life radically, but not frantically; without compromise, but with pastoral wisdom. At first, the disciples left all and followed Jesus, who "had nowhere to rest his head." They lived a life of homelessness much like the Hindu sannyasi or Buddhist bikshu, or mendicant monk. Yet even then, we still find Jesus and the disciples at Peter's house, sharing a meal with Peter's "mother-in-law," indicating that Peter still had a wife, a family, and a home. There must have been a balance that was accomplished by simple charity and love.

In the Acts of the Apostles, we see all the early Christians selling all their possessions and sharing "all things in common," so that there was "no poor among them." They distributed these goods "according to each one's need." This pastorally applies the strict itinerant and mendicant life of Jesus and the disciples to a larger group of people who live a more stable life in the city. It is radical. It is even considered extraordinary by today's standards. But it is still a pastoral application of the pure external ideal of Jesus and the disciples.

Finally, Saint Paul makes the ultimate pastoral application. Recognizing the strict renunciate poverty of Jesus, he allows the av-

erage Christian in Corinth to have possessions and wealth, stipu-
lating that they must share with the poor just short of impoverish-
ing themselves and their families. Yet even here he says the result
is "equality" between rich and poor. This is no perfunctory giving
to the poor. It is not minimal. It is so substantial that it actually
equalizes rich and poor. This is still quite radical by the standards
of today, when "rich Christians in an age of hunger" is the norm in
the developed world.

So the renunciation of the real disciple of Jesus is not externally identical in everyone. But it is still to be radical and real. It
must have "teeth" if it is to take a bite out of our radically disori-
ented lifestyles from which we seek to be "saved." If we do not wish
renunciation, then perhaps we do not really think we need saving.
Perhaps we really think we're okay just as we are.

But this is not the case. We need salvation. We need rebirth and
enlightenment. Jesus offers this to anyone who wishes to follow. To
follow, we must be real disciples. To be real disciples, we must renounce all and everything in a way that is appropriate, radical, and
wise. We must be willing to die to everything—every possession
and relationship, every word and action, every thought and emotion, even to our very self. Then we will be reborn and set free.
Then we will begin to walk the real way of the real Jesus.

# Called to Community

THERE IS A SPECIAL MOMENT DURING SOME OF MY CONCERTS that becomes a powerful symbol of the connection and unity we can experience in fellowship with one another. That's the time when everyone stands up, holds hands, and sings the words to the song, "Saint Theresa's Prayer":

> *"Christ has no body now but yours*
> *No hands, no feet on earth but yours*
> *Yours are the eyes through which He looks*
> *Compassion on this world*
> *Yours are the feet with which he walks*
> *To do good*
> *Yours are the hands with which He blesses*
> *All the world."*

As we sing this song together, it's amazing how the environment and energy of the room are transformed from a mere "concert performance" to a dynamic spiritual experience. Our sense of communal Christian unity becomes even more pronounced as hundreds or thousands of us sing the song's chorus together:

> *"Yours are the hands*
> *Yours are the feet*
> *Yours are the eyes*
> *You are His Body."*

As we hold hands and sing, people begin to see beyond the apparent reality of the evening to the eternal reality of Jesus in the hands of their brothers and sisters.

For me, experiences like this are powerful reminders of the power and presence of the Church, a body that is both physical and spiritual, now present and eternally alive. Just as in the Eucharist, where worshipers look beyond the apparent realities of bread and wine to see the real presence of Jesus, so in church we look beyond human frailties and limitations to the wonder of God's redemptive love in our lives.

During such moments of transcendent fellowship, we can see past the apparent ups and downs, successes and failures, holiness and sin of our brothers and sisters to see the real presence of Jesus in them. It's not magic or sorcery. It's simply God fulfilling his promise to be present in every person and every situation for those that have the "eyes to see."

Holding hands is such a simple act, but it is also profound. When we hold one another's hands, we can see Jesus in each and every person whom God has made and loves so deeply.

Saint Francis taught that if we approach the Eucharist with the eyes of flesh alone, all we will see is bread and wine, but if we look with the eyes of faith, we see Jesus' body and blood. It's much the same as we look upon our brothers and sisters in Christ. With our natural eyes, we may see only their outward appearance, talents, and shortcomings. With the eyes of faith, however, we see Jesus himself in our fellow disciples. Only when we see Jesus in others do we have the real authority to impart Jesus to everyone we meet. Otherwise, we run the risk of being judgmental and self-righteous.

Holding hands also symbolizes that we will hold one another up when we fall. All of us fall sooner or later. Only by holding one another's hands in community can we help one another along the way. Instead of letting go of others so we can move faster alone, we graciously slow down and wait. Then we gently but firmly help one another up and help others get started back along the way.

Community is like that when it breaks through from the human level to the Spirit. Such spiritual fellowship is a help. It is a joy. It enables our faith to grow beyond the superficial, childlike things of religion to the deeper and eternal things of the Spirit.

We have a saying in our community that the most important factor influencing whether or not a person will make it with us is not whether or not they share the big vision or calling to community, but whether they can take that big vision and calling and make it work in the innumerable little and ordinary things of life. This is the goal and purpose of real Christian community.

## SPIRITUALITY AS PERSONAL AND COMMUNAL

WHEN JESUS WALKED this earth, he called a group of disciples to follow him. And as soon as each disciple personally accepted that call, he immediately found himself part of a group. The personal and individual experience of following Jesus almost immediately became communal. It became "church," or "ecclesia," or the "gathering" of people around their Lord.

After three short and exciting years together, Jesus left his disciples and went to the cross. But the first Christians still continued as a community. As Chapter 24 of Luke tells us, before the discovery of the Resurrection, the followers of Jesus were assembled in one place. And after Jesus' Ascension into heaven, they were frequently together in the Temple.

The Book of Acts, also written by Luke, describes how this ragtag group of followers gradually became a more cohesive fellowship. They gathered together in the Upper Room, the place where the first Eucharist was instituted and celebrated by Jesus. They were together before and during the outpouring of the Holy Spirit at Pentecost. And they continued in intentional and radical community, even after the Spirit empowered evangelists to preach the new Gospel of Jesus to other towns, regions, and nations. As a result of this preaching, new communities immediately sprang up, and as these new fellowships were organized and overseen by the apostles, there was a growing sense that the Church—the mystical Body of Christ—was becoming a worldwide reality.

Today, Jesus calls each one of us both to himself and to his body, his community, his Church. When we enter the sanctuary to worship God, we are not alone. Many of God's children are in the room with us, and some of them people who because of their social, cultural, racial, or ethnic differences from us aren't the kinds of people we would typically associate with. But here they are with us, worshiping God together and revealing the awesome diversity of the family of God.

Some of us are raised in Christian families, through which we are baptized as infants and brought into a faith community at an early age. Others grow up without hearing about God but make an adult decision to follow Christ. Either way, sooner or later each one of us must make a personal decision about our faith in Jesus and our personal relationship with him. But as soon as we do this, we immediately find ourselves with a group—a community of people who have made that same individual choice to follow Jesus. Thus, our personal and individual faith in Jesus becomes a communal experience as well.

## CREATION IS COMMUNAL

ONE CAN FIND plenty of examples of community, cooperation, and interdependence throughout the natural world, where animals, plants, and even the tiniest microscopic organisms work together in complex ecosystems for the common good.

Most of the world's societies have a communal orientation toward life as well. Although the individual is important, residents of most nations believe the individual is best served by being in community, tribe, or family first. If the group prospers, the individual prospers and is kept safe and secure.

In 1978 I went on a pilgrimage to the Holy Land, and while there I met an Asian family in which the oldest son had had a chance to move away and start a business. In the West, he would be urged to do so and considered a hero if he succeeded. In the East, however, the hero is the one who stays at home and helps the whole family succeed. The son, therefore, stayed near his family, helping them to prosper along with him.

Of course, some societies have placed too little value on the individual's importance and rights. This can lead to excess and injustice. But the West has often gone too in the opposite direction, and I see the example of the East as a healthy balance.

Most major world religions exhibit a balance between personal and communal expressions of faith. Hindus, for example, have their ashrams, or communities, as a natural development of the disciple/guru relationship. Buddhists take refuge not only in the Buddha, or enlightenment, and the dharma, or the teaching, but also in the sangha, or the community, as well. Taoists and Confucianists emphasize not only the personal instruction and example of the sage-teacher, but the communal dimension of the disciples as well.

It's only in the modern, industrialized West that individualism has come to be revered above community. Capitalism, with its emphasis on competition rather than cooperation, has played a major role in this shift. Western philosophy and public policy have also often accentuated the rights of the individual over those of the collective whole.

The effort to understand the proper relationship between the one and the many—both spiritually and politically—has occupied the best minds of philosophy and theology for centuries.

The Franciscan theologian and philosopher John Duns Scotus (1266–1308) put forward the theory of "individuation." This theory recognized the uniqueness of each human soul as an unrepeatable and precious gift from God, but it viewed the individual within the greater context of the "interdependence" of creation, humanity, and the Church—all of which are totally dependent on God. I believe Duns Scotus achieved a healthy balance between individual and community, and key points of his theory have been affirmed by both Vatican II (in the 1960s) and Pope John Paul II.

Modern individualism, however, is individuation gone too far—a potentially good thing gone bad. And the impact on religious practice has been profound.

Few recent books have been so insightful, or had so great an impact, as *Habits of the Heart*, a book coauthored by Robert Bellah and published in 1985. The book's subtitle, "Individualism and

Commitment in Modern Life," hints at its subject: how the Western emphasis on individualism has had a debilitating effect on communal spirit in all aspects of life—including family, business, and religion.

Individualism is tearing down society as we know it. When self becomes our real god, all else is in danger. Families are falling apart, with only 32 percent of marriages staying together. The job force is always changing, with the average family relocating every four and a half years. Churches and communities of the Church find themselves unable to create and maintain the deeper and more stable aspects of Christian life and ministry, because of personnel turnover.

A bishop once told me that when he ordains a person for the ministry, he must do so with the intention that ordination is for life—and the person being ordained must have a life commitment too. But the "personnel director" in him must always be ready for them to last an average of only ten years.

He also said that in the "good old days," if a priest was discerning some kind of transfer, or leaving the active priesthood, he would come in and humbly lay out the situation before the bishop. The bishop would no doubt first try to get the man to stay by embracing the cross. If after some time this all failed, a dispensation was usually sought from Rome, and granted.

Today, however, the priest comes in with the canon law book under one arm and the civil law book under the other to demand his rights and win his case by intimidation. The bishop dare not encourage the person to "embrace the cross" for fear of being sued for mental abuse. A situation like this is outside the help of the classical religion of Christianity. It is imprisoned by the demon of self.

This is merely one example of how far we have been led astray by our worship of the false god of self at the temple of individualism.

## COMMUNITY AS MYSTICAL REALITY

TODAY, SPIRITUAL SEEKERS around the world are experiencing a hunger for strong and ancient religious roots. As these pilgrims find their way back to Judaism, Christianity, Islam, and various Eastern faiths, they encounter this call to community.

Regardless of whether these seekers are coming from a New Age approach, or from a seeker-sensitive "mega-church" down the street, one of the first things they must confront—perhaps for the first time—is their deep commitment to individualism, and their exaltation of personal freedom above all else.

Certainly, Christianity confronts them with a clear challenge: the old worship of self must die, so that a new communal orientation toward God, church, and all of life can be reborn. And paradoxically, through letting go of self-worship, the true self will be reborn and set free. But there is also a mystical dimension of this letting go that we must see.

I have seen many individuals become Catholics and even join intentional communities like ours, the Brothers and Sisters of Charity. But I have observed that unless they make their commitment to community a mystical reality that pervades their entire lives, the process will be reduced to a futile practice of rules and legalism, and this is an approach that will ultimately result in failure. For when they encounter the inevitable human flaws in the Church, or in our community, they will simply give up after the initial experience of newness and excitement wears off.

God must become reality to us if community is to work. He must cease to simply be a religious concept or an outside force. We must stop seeing things in terms of "me" and "him." He must simply "be." It's that "being" within us that will cause us to be reborn.

It is God with us and within us that will make community a joy and help us on our way. Community will become "communion," or "common union," in and through this deeper reality of Christ. Then the difficulties of community become opportunities to look deeper to find the common ground of experience with every other brother or sister, no matter how different they may be from us through culture or temperament. We become a team when we are all experiencing this deeper reality of God.

## MYSTICAL MEETS PRACTICAL

COMMUNITY IS NOT some kind of otherworldly experience. It is spiritual *and* physical. It is mystical *and* practical.

Some would argue that because Jesus promised his followers that the Spirit would lead us to all truth, leadership was no longer necessary. Everyone would live in perfect harmony and peace because all would be perfectly hearing and inspired by the Spirit of God. Right?

Wrong. We do not live in a perfect world, even after Jesus. Redemption is now, but still in progress. It is "already, but not yet." Even the best-meaning and most-intelligent Christians do not always properly discern the authentic working of the Spirit. Sometimes, we get it wrong.

Looking into scripture, we can see that as soon as there was a "community" of disciples gathered around Jesus, he began establishing order and leadership. Jesus could not be equally intimate with everyone who followed him, but rather had a closer relationship with "the three": Peter, James, and John. They were with him during times of urgent, intimate prayer, such as the day they spent upon the Mount of Transfiguration (MATTHEW 17), or the night of final agony in the Garden of Gethsemane (MATTHEW 26).

Next came the twelve (which included the three). These men

were close enough to be constant traveling companions, but not all could be Jesus' best friends. Then there were the seventy-two disciples (LUKE 10), who were often sent ahead of Jesus and the twelve to prepare each village for his arrival. These spent even less intimate time with Jesus than did the twelve or the three, but they played an important role in his ministry.

And under God's guidance, the first Christians imposed a God-ordained structure on their growing movement. In doing so, they were exhibiting a tendency that can be seen throughout creation. Most societies among living creatures have a leadership structure and one specific leader. Packs have a pecking order and a final leader. Bees have workers, leaders, and an ultimate queen bee. Among humans, tribes have councils, and every council has a chief. Nations have parliaments and prime ministers, or a congress and a president. The Jews had elders and then Moses. Later, they had a Sanhedrin and a high priest. If leaders are bad, systems work badly. But most of the time at least some system is necessary for civilization to function. Without it, there is not only division but chaos. That chaos is not the will of God. Saint Paul says simply, "[God] is not the God of disorder but of peace" (1 CORINTHIANS 14:33).

The apostles, all of whom had known and served Christ personally, continued as leaders under the direction of James and Peter. One of the first items of business for the apostles was replacing Judas, who had committed suicide after betraying Jesus. After fasting and praying, they chose Mathias as Judas's successor.

It makes perfect sense that those who knew Jesus best while he was alive would lead and shepherd the Church after his death and Resurrection. They had been Jesus' most devoted students, and thus played an important role in preserving the true character of the master's teaching, protecting the believers from heresy and error, as well as from false spirits and prophets, which are sometimes called "anti-Christs" in the Bible. These early Christian leaders even developed a name for the care they lavished on preserving the true teaching of Jesus: they called it "discernment."

In Acts, we regularly read about how the earliest Christians "devoted themselves to the teaching of the apostles and to the communal life, to the breaking of the bread and to the prayers" (ACTS 2:42). Miracles and blessings were experienced by nearly everyone, but the apostles were recognized as having a preeminent role in this ministry.

When property and goods were sold or distributed to the poor, everyone would first "lay them at the feet of the apostles to distribute to everyone according to his need" (ACTS 4). When Ananias and Sapphira, a couple in the Church, attempted to deceive the other believers by holding back some of their possessions from the common purse, it was the apostles—specifically Peter, who was their leader—who was given supernatural discernment to uncover this fraud, which was not committed primarily against the apostles and the other believers but against the Spirit of God himself (ACTS 5:1–11)!

As the church—and the demands of leadership—grew, the apostles appointed seven assistants, called deacons. They were commissioned when the apostles laid their hands on them and blessed them (ACTS 6).

In the decades after Jesus' death and resurrection, this is how the early church was organized by God's grace. The apostles, who recognized Peter as their leader, stood between God and the growing number of believers, seeking to lead with love, humility, and sensitivity to the Spirit.


## CONTINUITY THROUGH SUCCESSION

JUST AS THE APOSTLES appointed deacons, they also appointed leaders in the many churches that were beginning to spring up as the Christian message was spread around the world. And in every case, the apostles appointed these new leaders by the laying on of hands, just as they had with the deacons.

This was even the case with Saul, the man who once persecuted the Church before converting to the faith of Christ and changing his name to Paul. Even this man, who is called simply "the Apostle" by tradition, submitted himself to the apostles who came before him for authentic discernment and confirmation. He had a personal encounter with and vision of Jesus. Jesus spoke directly to him about his mission. He also spent extended time in the solitude of Arabia to mature spiritually. Even with this experiential authority, Saint Paul went up to Jerusalem to meet first with Peter and James. After fourteen years, he says,

> I again went up to Jerusalem with Barnabas, taking Titus along also. I went up in accord with a revelation, and I presented to them the gospel that I preach to the Gentiles—but privately to those of repute—so that I might not be running, or have run, in vain. . . . and when they recognized the grace bestowed upon me, James and Kephas and John, who were reputed to be pillars, gave me and Barnabas their right hands in partnership [GALATIANS 2:1–2, 9].

From that day to this, the faith has been passed down from those who knew, lived with, and touched Jesus. And it has been through touch that Church leadership has been passed on for twenty centuries. That process of passing on leadership—from the first apostles to the present priests, bishops, and other leaders—is called apostolic succession.

The writings of the early church leaders speak often of apostolic succession, and particularly of the special role of the bishop of Rome, who was successor to Peter, the one who had long been esteemed as the first among the apostles.

Saint Clement of Rome, an important early successor to Saint Peter, wrote these words some time between A.D. 80 and 101:

> The apostles received the gospel for us from the Lord Jesus Christ; and Jesus Christ was sent by God. . . . Through countryside and city they preached; and appointed their earliest converts . . . to be bishops and deacons. . . . Our apostles knew through our Lord Jesus Christ that there would be strife for the office of the bishop. For this reason . . . they appointed those already mentioned, and afterwards added . . . if they should die other approved men should succeed to their ministry . . .

Saint Ignatius of Antioch, who lived from approximately A.D. 35–107, wrote frequently on the subjects of Church leadership and apostolic succession. In his letter to the Magnesians, he instructs these believers to:

> Do all things in harmony with God, with the bishop presiding in the place of God and with the presbyters [priests] in the place of the council of the Apostles, and with the deacons, who are most dear to me, entrusted with the business of Jesus Christ.

To the Trallians, Ignatius wrote, "Without these [bishops, priests, and deacons], it cannot be called church." And to the Philadelphians, he says:

> Take care to use one Eucharist . . . for there is one flesh of our Lord Jesus Christ and one cup in the union of his blood; one altar, as there is one bishop with the presbytery and my fellow servants, the deacons. . . . Do nothing without the bishop. . . . love unity, flee divisions. I did my best as a man devoted to unity.

Finally, to the Smyrnaeans, Ignatius writes:

> *Follow the bishop as Jesus Christ follows the Father.*
> *Reverence the deacons as . . . the command of God. Let no one*
> *do anything of concern to the church without the bishop. Let that*
> *be considered a valid Eucharist which is celebrated by the bishop,*
> *or by one he appoints.*

From this brief review of scripture and early Church writings, we can clearly see that this apostolic succession was an important link between Jesus and the many who would later come to believe in him. Succession provided a way for people who lived long after the death and Resurrection of Jesus to touch the Incarnate Word through his Body on earth—the Church. Thus divinity was manifested and revealed in an extraordinary way through humanity. And thanks to apostolic succession, the Church continues to share in this wonderful mystery through his love, his grace, and his mercy.

The Church of Jesus Christ is more than an institution with a rule book and leaders. Businesses have that, but the Church has the living Spirit of Jesus himself. Christians are "living stones [in a] spiritual house" (1 PETER 2:5), writes Peter. Or as Paul says, believers are:

> *the household of God, built upon the foundation of the apos-*
> *tles and the prophets, with Christ Jesus himself as the cornerstone*
> [EPHESIANS 2:19–20].

Further, through baptism, we all share in something the Church calls "the priesthood of all believers." Each of us has equal dignity before God and is given an equally important calling on our life.

Not all of us are ordained to be deacons, priests, or bishops, however. Although these ordained servants have a unique role, that does not excuse all of us from finding our calling and serving God with all our hearts.

This is a mystical reality that requires us to look beyond the person of the bishop or his priest or deacon and see the Incarnate Christ in and through all that is appropriately taught and commanded. We learn how to see God in humanity, the divine in and through the human, the infallible through the fallible, the perfect through the flawed. We then see Jesus in every member of the Church, the Body of Christ, which has been handed down to us from the apostles themselves. It is then that we can truly sing together, "You are His Body."

## THE PLACE OF PETER

JESUS CHOSE PETER from among the twelve apostles for a unique and special role of leadership (MATTHEW 16 and JOHN 21). Peter maintained his primary role during the important years that the early Church was being established and Christianity was being spread throughout the world, and he became the bishop of the Church in the all-important city of Rome.

Over the centuries, as the Church continued to grow, the bishop of Rome took on an increasingly important role in shepherding this growing flock.

Ignatius of Antioch, who was one of the primary early Church leaders, referred to the Roman church as the one "which holds the presidency" among other churches. And Saint Iranaeus of Lyons (A.D. 140–202) said the church in Rome played a powerful role. He called it "the greatest and most ancient church known to all . . . that church which has the tradition and the faith which comes down to us after having been announced to men by the apostles. For with this church, because of its superior origin, all churches must agree." By around A.D. 200, Tertullian was calling the bishop of Rome the "Vicar of Christ," who was seen as the keeper of unity and truth.

Around A.D. 250, Saint Cyprian of Carthage wrote, "There is one God and one Christ and one church and one chair founded on Peter by the word of the Lord. It is not possible to set up another altar or . . . another priesthood."

Soon, the church began calling the bishop of Rome the Pope, a term which may sound formal and official to us, but which comes from the word "papa." Saint Leo I the Great, who served as Pope from A.D. 440–61 wrote the following:

> *In individual provinces there should be individual bishops whose opinion among their brothers should be first, and again, certain others, established in larger cities, were to accept a greater responsibility. Through them, the care of the universal church would converge in the one See of Peter, and nothing should ever be at odds with this head.*

I could obviously include many other quotes here, but I think I have sufficiently illustrated the point that just as Peter had a special role in Jesus' life, those who succeeded Peter as bishop of Rome had a special role in the worldwide church. Even though four other major churches were founded by apostles (Jerusalem, Antioch, Alexandria, and Constantinople), Rome always held the preeminent place, even after the secular capitol of the empire moved from Rome to Constantinople (and thus insuring the proper separation between religious and secular authorities).

Because the Catholic Church is the inheritor of centuries of

tradition, it has been able to enjoy a fullness, a unity, and a tradition that other Christian bodies have never had. It's not that we're
better than other Christians. It's just that we're able to receive and
appreciate the fullness of God, as passed down from the first apostles until now.

Let's contrast, for a moment, this long lineage of spiritual tradition with the disunity and infighting that has plagued the
Protestant churches which grew out of the Protestant Reformation
of the sixteenth century.

The desire of the Reformers was to restore the church to its earlier glory. And all people agree that the Church of the fifteenth and
sixteenth centuries was in need of restoration. But in breaking free
of the chain of succession that had stretched from Christ to their
own day, the Reformers unintentionally created a domino effect of
division, which has plagued the past four hundred years of Christian
history. Time after time, one group after another has broken away
from their Protestant parent bodies to form a newer and supposedly
better church. Today, there are literally thousands of Christian denominations, each one claiming to be true to the Gospel, but each
one lacking the apostolic authority that still resides in the Catholic
Church. History has clearly revealed the terrible effects of this divisive approach.

There are squabbles within the Catholic Church as well, but in
spite of these differences Catholics remain the largest united body
of Christians in the world, and their universally recognized leader
is the pope. No other religious leader alive today carries as much authority as the pope. No other popular preacher, healer, or saint
draws such huge crowds, and no one is listened to as closely—by
Catholics, other religious people, unbelievers, and secular business
and political leaders. The current pope has helped shape history,
bringing social and political change—for example, in the former
Communist bloc countries of Eastern Europe and in Cuba.

The pope has also worked to bring representatives of all Christian churches and world religions closer together through appropriate dialogue, humble repentance, and simple prayer. He has done this in a way that respects the uniqueness of each person's beliefs and their common right to religious liberty. Most important, he continues to preach the Gospel of Jesus Christ around the globe, which contributes to the Catholic Christian Church being one of the fastest-growing religious bodies on the face of the earth.

The pope would not be "papa" without the one billion people he represents, nor would the people be so united without the pope. The media follows him on every trip he takes and reports on every major speech he gives. This in itself is a testimony to the fact that Roman Catholic Christianity works as the most effective corporate body of believers on earth.

If the pope and the Christian tradition he represents are so powerful, why aren't more people Catholic? It's simple. Roman Catholic Christianity isn't perfect, even though it has received two gifts from God: "indefectibility" and "infallibility."

In layman's terms, indefectibility means we just "muddle through" most of the time. Only under certain clear conditions and great anointing of the Holy Spirit does God occasionally grace us with infallibility, and then only. At other times, popes, bishops, and laity are just sinners saved by grace. We mess up and we often need forgiveness. I am encouraged by the fact that modern popes have asked forgiveness for helping cause the Protestant Reformation, and for persecuting Galileo. These are just a few of the major blunders for which the pope and the Church have desperately needed God's and humanity's forgiveness.

Frankly, there are times when I think it's a miracle for someone to become a Catholic (as I did!). It's a challenge to see infallibility in such a fallible organization. That's why we need God's grace to achieve the unity he desires us to enjoy.

There's a powerful passage in the Gospel of John, Chapter 17, where Jesus says that if the Church is not united in love, the world will not believe that the Father sent Jesus to the world to redeem us. Today we can see the truth of Jesus' words, for by and large we are not united, and by and large, the world does not believe.

The history of Christianity contains many regretful episodes of hurt and division. Often, such division and disunity have been God's efforts to chastise or correct the church for its wrongdoing. Such painful periods cause us to hold steady and true to the things we know to be from God, even in the face of trial and persecution. They also call us to deep and genuine repentance and conversion when we have either not done God's will or have missed God's will by doing the right thing in the wrong way, of doing the things of Christ in an un-Christlike manner. Such failures, which are all too common, are part of why both Vatican II and Pope John Paul II have said that all genuine Christian ecumenism must begin with a deep and profound repentance on the part of all participants for the part they or their forebears played in causing the present division among Christians.

## THE CALL TO COMMUNION

CATHOLIC CHRISTIAN spirituality teaches that we are called not only to "union" with Christ, but "common union," or "communion," with and in Christ. Salvation, rebirth, and enlightenment are not only deeply personal but also corporate and communal. We are a body.

This communal oneness includes the doctrine and teaching of the mind, the devotional and contemplative mystery of the heart, and the structural unity and coordination of the bones, sinews, and muscles of the body. But the members must be healthy in order for the whole body to be healthy. This places value on the individual person, but always in the context of the greater community. It creates a sense of individuation and interdependence that is at odds with the rampant individualism and false independence of the contemporary West.

Christ's Body creates a sense of community and extended family that stands in sharp contrast to the unraveling of even the most basic communal and familial structures through the breakdown of values and genuine commitment.

But the emphasis on the larger universal and global dimensions and structures of the Catholic Church does not diminish the proper emphasis on both the intimately personal dimension of spirituality and holiness, and the movements and communities within the larger community of the Church that emphasize a particular charism—or ministry—in a beautiful and splendid way.

Beginning with the earliest experience of the communal Church, individuals went into solitude and silence to discover a deeper and more intense personal experience of God. This gave birth to the whole monastic experience, as others followed the same call or example of a holy man or woman. First, colonies of solitaries were formed, and then these colonies developed into fully organized communities that exemplified the whole Gospel life in a more intense and perfected way. Then these same communities overflowed into active ministries. These ministries gave birth to the whole heritage of religious or consecrated life that continues to develop and unfold within the Church to this very day.

A good example of the evolution of communities is Saint Benedict himself, the "father of Western monasticism." When he lived as a hermit, he considered solitude so important that he almost missed the Church's celebration of Easter, the most important feast of the liturgical year. Yet he went on to form a very organized expression of communal monasticism that places much emphasis on communal and corporate prayer.

The Church uses the phrase "succession of the saints" to refer to people like Saint Benedict and Saint Francis, who emphasized personal holiness, union with God, and ministry to the Church and the world. Many of these saints gave birth to "communities within the community of the Church," which have been important complements and completions to the more general and universal covering of the Catholic Church.

## SHEEP WITHOUT A SHEPHERD

The saga of division and disunity in the Church over the centuries is strikingly similar to the dispersion and regathering of the Jews in the Hebrew Bible. According to scripture, the Jews were dispersed because of their own sins, and particularly the sins of their leaders. As Ezekiel the Prophet said:

> they were scattered for lack of a shepherd, and became food for all the wild beasts. My sheep were scattered and wandered over all the mountains and high hills; my sheep were scattered over the whole earth, with no one to look after them or to search for them.
>
> Therefore, shepherds, hear the word of the Lord. . . . because my shepherds did not look after my sheep, but pastured themselves and did not pasture my sheep; because of this . . . I swear I am coming against these shepherds. I will claim my sheep from them and put a stop to their shepherding my sheep so that they may no longer pasture themselves . . . I myself will look after and tend my sheep. As a shepherd tends his flock when he finds himself

*among his scattered sheep, so will I tend my sheep . . . In good
pastures will I pasture them . . . I myself will pasture my sheep;
I myself will give them rest, says the Lord God* [EZEKIEL
34:5–15].

God did not forsake the sheep, but devised a new way of relating with them, replacing the old priesthood and Temple sacrificial system with new leadership and new forms of worship. A
new synagogue system was led by rabbis, or mostas. In a departure
from the tradition that had governed the priesthood, rabbis could
come from any lineage, so now the Spirit could raise up anyone to
study under a rabbi and be recognized as ready to be a rabbi himself.

The Jewish people prospered, both spiritually and physically,
under this new system of synagogue and rabbi. Over time, the Jews
became an increasingly important and respected part of the various
communities in which they found themselves.

Then came the prophets' call for God's people to gather once
again in the homeland. Nehemiah, Ezra, and other prophets called
the Jewish people to return to Jerusalem, rebuild its walls, restore
the Temple, and reestablish both the original priesthood and the
Temple sacrifices and worship. The synagogue system and rabbis
were not abandoned but were incorporated into the ongoing regathering and restoration. But still, many Jews remained in the
places of their dispersion, preferring to enjoy their newfound success rather than returning to the barren wasteland from which they
had come.

I believe there are some striking parallels between this brief
overview of the later cycles of Jewish history and the story of the
Christian Church.

God established an original "homeland" of lifestyle, leadership, and worship for the Church. We believers had our priesthood through apostolic succession and the successors to Peter, the Vicar of Christ. We had our temple sacrifice in the Eucharist. We had a lifestyle, or city walls, built squarely on the lives of Jesus, the apostles, and the saints.

But in time the Church fell into sin. The leaders began to feed themselves instead of God's flock. So God chastised them by dispensing the flock and raising up new shepherds to show them all that he alone was the ultimate Good Shepherd. What is the new system? Who are those shepherds?

The Protestant Reformation is that new "synagogue," which is centered not on temple sacrifice or the Eucharist but on the Word. And the Protestant nonpriestly ministers are the new "rabbis," who are no longer dependent on lineage or succession but only on the Spirit and good training.

In short, God raised up the Reformation to chastise the abuses of both laity and leadership within the Roman Catholic Christian community, and to show everyone clearly that he and he alone was the ultimate Good Shepherd and primate of the church.


## THE REGATHERING

I BELIEVE THAT today I can hear God issuing a further call to Regathering and Restoration—a call to many in the Protestant tradition to return home to Rome, to rediscover the ancient richness and beauty of apostolic succession, the reality of the Holy Eucharist, and the communion of the saints of God.

One can see a preview of this regathering in the last century with the Oxford Movement and Saint John Henry Newman. It continues today with so-called "evangelical Catholics" like Dale Vree, Thomas Howard, Dan O'Neill, and even myself, to name just a few.

This regathering incorporates the blessing gained from the Protestant Reformation of the sixteenth century as well as the Orthodox schism of the eleventh century. These important milestones must not be forgotten or abandoned for the sake of unity with Rome. Instead, the uniqueness and blessings of each Christian tradition and community must remain substantially intact as they are integrated into the greater unity within the fold of the Roman homeland.

One can see this regathering happening already as clergy from Protestant churches are being reordained as Catholic priests. There are also entire Protestant congregations that are being received into the Catholic Church. Both clergy and congregations maintain their unique personalities and gifts, and in some cases new liturgies are being created for these new, regathered fellowships.

The outlines of this regathering are powerful and exciting. They are nothing short of prophetic and revolutionary. May we all pray for the wonderful work of Christian ecumenism, regathering, and restoration.

Such work takes great patience. Already, many Christians around the world sense a unity of heart. Unity of mind and organizational structure are still a long way off, however. That's why it's so important for people of faith to engage in intentional, careful, and mutually respectful dialogue. Dialogue certainly clarifies areas of disagreement, but it can also break down walls of mistrust and misunderstanding between believers from different Christian communities.

Perhaps it will take a miracle to put the Church back together again. But let's not leave it all to God. Human beings helped cause the deep divisions in Christ's body, and it will take human beings to heal these divisions through the practice of authentic and genuine Christianity on all sides once again.

I don't know if I will see the final regathering of the Church in my lifetime. God has shown me that I will see the promised land only from afar. In the meantime, I can do my part and pray that my own stupidity and foolishness do not contribute to greater division and misunderstanding. Let us all pray for the patience and the perseverance to complete this urgent work.

# Guided by
# the Spirit

I LOVE HEARING A MUSICIAN GIVING AN INSPIRED PERFOR-
mance. At these times, the musician and the music become one,
lifting the listener to a moving, even transcendent aesthetic experience.

Music like this is in sharp contrast to the dull, machine-like
performances some musicians give. The notes are all there, and
everything is played with total precision, but there's a certain something missing. Though technically proficient, such performances
are soulless.

Christianity can sometimes seem the same way. Believers may
be able to quote chapter and verse, and they may have all the mo-
tions down, but like robot musicians, they're missing the spirit of
the thing, for Christianity is much more than a set of wise teachings. It is living, supernatural truth. Christianity is more than creed

and code, it is communion with the Spirit of the living God. In this chapter, we will talk about how we can truly experience the reality and vibrancy of the spiritual life.

## A SPIRITUAL HERITAGE

ONE OF THE MOST important books of the 1960s was Harvey Cox's groundbreaking work *The Secular City*, which boldly predicted the imminent demise of religion and the rise of secularism. But by 1995, Cox had changed his tune, as we can see in his book *Fire from Heaven: The Rise of Pentecostal Spirituality and the Reshaping of Religion in the Twenty-first Century.*

The Pentecostal movement is a powerful twentieth-century phenomenon. Pentecostalism, which emphasizes ecstatic religious experiences and divine miracles, was born in the early 1900s in places like California, Kansas, and Arkansas. But scholars say this movement, which began with only a few dozen enthusiastic worshipers, should soon balloon to half a billion Pentecostal and charismatic believers around the world.

Pentecostals get their name from the day of Pentecost, which was the day on which the Christian Church was born:

> When the time for Pentecost was fulfilled, they were all in one place together. And suddenly there came from the sky a noise like a strong driving wind, and it filled the entire house in which they were. Then there appeared to them tongues as of fire, which parted and came to rest on each one of them. And they were all filled with the Holy Spirit [ACTS OF THE APOSTLES, 2:1–4].

Today, people may not commonly think of the Catholic Church as Pentecostal, but it is. No Pentecostal or charismatic preacher has ever "out-Pentecostaled" Saint Peter or Saint Paul, the first pope and missionary apostle of the Catholic Church! What's even more interesting to some is the fact that today the Catholic Charismatic Renewal movement, of which I am a part, constitutes the largest single and fully united body of Pentecostals among Christians in the world. With approximately ten million participants, its numbers far exceed those of even the largest non-Catholic charismatic denomination, the Assemblies of God, with four million members.

Unfortunately, the church often seems stillborn, or just plain "dead on its feet" in many places today. The Spirit was given to the whole Church at Pentecost and to each member at Baptism and Confirmation, but we don't always know how to receive this gift.

Sadly, this has resulted in competition and "turf wars" between Pentecostals and Catholics, especially in such traditionally Catholic areas as Central and South America, where Pentecostal churches are growing rapidly and Catholic churches are in a state of numerical decline. This has upset some Catholic leaders, whose zeal to reclaim lost members has unfortunately led to some un-Christlike behavior. But for years I have been saying that the Catholic Church shouldn't focus on the fact that Pentecostals are "stealing" its members. Instead, it should seek to understand why they are stealable!

In other words, I believe Catholics are going over to non-Catholic Pentecostalism because we Catholics have not been Pentecostal enough. After all, Pentecost is part of our tradition and heritage, too. It is part of the succession of the saints we honor. Perhaps it is time for us to rediscover this vital and important element of our own Catholic tradition. Perhaps it is time for us to be more fully Pentecostal.

## "POWER FROM ON HIGH"

JESUS CALLED HIS disciples, gathered them into a community, walked with them and taught them for years, and established an apostolic leadership among them which soon became the leadership for the early church. But even after Jesus had given them all this preparation, he did not believe they had all that they needed to fully be the Church, the gathering of God's people.

The disciples had renounced all to follow Christ, had heard their master preach and teach, and had seen him work miracles, cast out devils, heal the sick, and even raise the dead! They had witnessed his crucifixion and death, as well as his Resurrection from the dead and his Ascension to the right hand of the Father in heaven. But even though they had seen and personally lived and experienced all of this, Jesus did not believe they yet had all of the inspiration and empowerment they would eventually need to fully face the big bad world with the good news of his Gospel message. What did they still lack?

Jesus said they still lacked the full anointing of the Holy Spirit. In his closing words from Luke's Gospel, Jesus tells his disciples: "Wait . . . for the fulfillment of my Father's promise, of which you have heard me speak." Luke continues this theme in the opening passage of the Acts of the Apostles:

> in a few days, you will be baptized with the Holy Spirit. . . . You
> will receive power when the Holy Spirit comes upon you; and you
> will be my witnesses in Jerusalem, throughout Judea and Samaria,
> and to the ends of the earth [ACTS 1:5–8].

The Apostles had already received a special anointing of the Holy Spirit, which had enabled them to work miracles and forgive people's sins. But Jesus still needed to unloose the special baptism of the Spirit that would be common to all believers—a special power that would see them through the incredible trials and tribulations, tests and persecutions that they were about to face. Jesus knew they needed a powerful and unquestionable outpouring of the Holy Spirit. That outpouring occurred at Pentecost.

Luke tells us the gift of the Spirit was accompanied by a physical sign—tongues of fire on each believer's head. In addition, he says, "They began to express themselves in foreign tongues and make bold proclamations as the Spirit prompted them." At the time, there were many Jewish people gathered in Jerusalem from around the region to celebrate the Feast of Pentecost, and these Jews spoke many different tongues and dialects. Yet Luke tells us that "each heard [the believers] speaking in his own language." The whole phenomenon was apparently pretty loud and boisterous, for a large crowd gathered to observe it, with some concluding that the uproar could have only been inspired by "secular" causes. "They have had too much wine," said some of these curious skeptics.

But the early Christians received far more than wine. They received the very power of God. And it was this power that enabled them to face their upcoming persecution with a calm peace and a solid courage that would shake the whole Western world. The young Church's apostles, preachers, and prophets would set an example for holiness and spiritual power that would make all the old religions of Greece, Rome, and the Middle East pale in comparison. The phenomenal growth and spread of the Christian faith wasn't the result of good preaching or public relations. Rather, it was an outgrowth of the power that came from God's gift of his Holy Spirit.

## THE SPIRIT BRINGS LIFE

WHEN GOD GAVE the gift of the Holy Spirit (capital "S") to the Church, this was in some ways similar to the way he gave the human spirit (small "s") to man and woman at the moment of creation. The Book of Genesis tells us that as God breathed life into the first man, "so man became a living being" (GENESIS 2:7). And at Pentecost, Luke tells us that accompanying the gift of the Holy Spirit there came "a noise like a strong driving wind" (ACTS 2:2).

The Spirit is the animating or "life-giving" reality in the Church. Without the Spirit, the Church may have substance and form, but it is not truly alive. It is dead. As God first formed Adam before he breathed life into him, so Jesus first formed the Church through a call to discipleship, teaching, and appointment of leaders before he sent the Spirit at Pentecost. It was only then that the Church came to life; only then that the Church was actually born. Without the Spirit, it would have been stillborn.

There are some important lessons we can learn from the way God gave his Spirit to the church:

First, all the believers were "gathered in one place." They were community, and received the gift of the Spirit as community.

But second, the tongues of the fire of the Spirit "came to rest on each of them. All were filled with the Holy Spirit." Thus this gift was not only corporate but also individual. It was for both "each" and "all." Pentecostalism is for the whole community, and each and every single member of it.

Throughout history well-meaning people have made many mistakes either by emphasizing the community to the point of nullifying the individual, or by emphasizing the individual experience of the Spirit to the danger and negation of the communal reality of experience and discernment. Both community and individual are clearly included in scripture, because both are important. What is needed is a harmony and balance between the two.

A third important point is that God gave the Spirit to his Church for ministry to others. It wasn't merely a gift to be enjoyed by the believers, but rather it was given to be shared with others.

Acts shows us that immediately after the Spirit was given to the believers, Peter stood up with the eleven apostles and preached a powerful sermon explaining both the Pentecostal experience of the Spirit and the ministry of Jesus as well. As a result, some three thousand accepted his message and received both baptism and the gift of the Spirit.

The powerful ministry did not stop there. The Spirit brought the believers back to a community that now had new power and enthusiasm. It also had great balance. It included apostolic instruction, communal life and commonly held goods, a sacramental experience of Eucharist, signs and wonders with apostolic discernment, and outreach to the existing people of the area.

Because these early believers were empowered by God's Spirit, they exhibited a great sincerity and joy that was attractive and infectious to others. Consequently, numerous people converted to the Christian faith and joined these enthusiastic believers in their communal life of following Jesus.

## RECEIVING THE GIFT

I BELIEVE THAT God still wants to give the gift of his Spirit to us today much as he gave it to the early Christians nearly two thousand years ago. But often, the problem is on our end. We don't want to receive God's gift.

Suppose I wanted to give a beautiful gift to Viola, my wife. I can offer it to her, but if she makes no effort to receive it by reaching out in some way, or opening her hands, the gift cannot be fully received, even though I made every effort to give it. Of course, I could just throw it at her, or dump it in her lap, but that could do damage to both the gift and her. Instead, I hold out the gift, waiting for her to make a response of some kind. Her willingness to receive my gift is a prerequisite to the gift being fully given with love and care.

It's the same with us. God is waiting to bless us with the gift of his Holy Spirit, but we must accept it. We must reach out with open hands to receive the Spirit before the gift can be fully effective in our life or in the life of the Church. The Spirit is given repeatedly by God to the Church and each member. We have not always fully received it, however.

How do we receive the gift of God's Spirit? The Scriptures give us four simple suggestions:

- First, we must ask God, through *prayer,* to give us his Spirit (LUKE 11:9–13).
- Second, through uninhibited *worship and praise* we can stir up our minds and hearts (PSALM 100).
- Third, expectant *faith* and real *forgiveness* open the way to the signs and wonders of the power of the Spirit (MARK 11:22–25).
- Last, and most important, a lifestyle of *letting go* of, or dying to, the old self and rising to the new person of the spirit is essential (GALATIANS 5:16–26).

These are some simple but powerful ways we can open ourselves to receive the gift of the Spirit.

## LIVING BY THE SPIRIT

OTHER THAN GIVING us a sense of empowerment and new life, what specifically does the Spirit do?

Most essentially, the Spirit brings the very person of Jesus into the very being of each believer. Earlier in this book we discussed the distinct but overlapping persons of the Trinity. The Spirit, which Saint Paul calls "the Spirit of Christ," is the normal vehicle through which Jesus, the Son, lives and dwells within us.

This is something very mystical and even somewhat mysterious.

Saint Paul says, "No one knows what pertains to God but the Spirit of God" (1 CORINTHIANS 2:11).

In the same passage, Paul says that through the gift of the Spirit, "we have the mind of Christ." What is this mind of Christ? Elsewhere, Paul explains this more completely:

*Have among yourselves the same attitude that is also yours in*
*Christ Jesus,*
*Who, though he was in the form of God,*
*did not regard equality with God something to be grasped.*
*Rather, he emptied himself,*
*taking the form of a slave,*
*coming in human likeness;*
*and found human in appearance,*
*he humbled himself,*
*becoming obedient to death, even death on a cross*
[PHILIPPIANS 2:5–8].

In an earlier chapter, we discussed discipleship, saying that "Christian" means to be "like Christ." Now we see that it is the Spirit that helps us be like Christ.

Often, Pentecostals and others have a quite different understanding of the role of the Spirit. They think being filled with the Spirit means being motivated or "fired up." One can be "fired up" and still not really be filled with God's Spirit, just as one can be excited about a football game, a political rally, or even a war. Even more subtly, one can be "fired up" about Christian faith and morality, praise and worship, signs and wonders, or mystical prayer and quiet contemplation, and still not really be "like Christ." We can worship the "gifts" and not the "Giver." We can do a Christian thing in an un-Christlike way.

Certainly, the presence of the Spirit can bring a certain level of enthusiasm to our spiritual life. In fact, the term "enthusiasm" comes from the root words *"en theos,"* or "of God." Therefore, true enthusiasm is of God. Yet false enthusiasm is superficial and short-lived if it fails to bring real transformation to our lives.

It is relatively easy to be enthusiastic when something is still novel and new, like a new romance or marriage. But true enthusiasm perseveres through the long haul, like a beautiful marriage that lasts through the normal ups and downs of life. It brings a love, a joy, and a peace that endure, even through sorrows and trials. Enthusiasm is like an inner fire that burns steady and sure through even the coldest time of winter. It is more than just a passing emotion, though it includes and directs our emotions in a healthy and positive way.

Historically, the Catholic Christian faith has always emphasized the transformative activities of the Spirit in our lives. For example, the Church's catechism emphasizes the following list of seven spiritual gifts, which are found in the Old Testament book of Isaiah: wisdom, understanding, counsel, fortitude, knowledge, piety, and fear of the Lord (CATECHISM 1831). Next, the catechism lists Paul's "fruit of the Spirit" (which are also found in GALATIANS 5:22–23): "charity, joy, peace, patience, kindness, goodness, generosity, gentleness, faithfulness, modesty, self-control, and chastity" (CATECHISM 1832).

I am reminded of a sign I once saw on a charismatic pastor's wall that read: "I want spiritual fruit, not religious nuts!" I believe God wants his Holy Spirit to make us more like Christ, not merely more excited or enthusiastic. God wants to empower us so we can do the "right thing rightly" and stop missing Christ while doing a Christian thing in an un-Christlike way. This is the real test of spiritual maturity.

There are also ministry-related gifts of the Spirit, which are given by God specifically for the building up of the Church and her mission to bring the Good News of Jesus Christ to all the world (see 1 Corinthians 12–14, where Saint Paul speaks of these "charismatic" gifts at length).

Some of these ministry gifts are rather simple and clear, like the gifts given to apostles, prophets, teachers, assistants, or administrators. Others—such as the gifts of healing, miracles, and speaking in tongues—are more controversial today.

These spiritual gifts can be abused. The Corinthians had an unfortunate tendency to misuse the more flamboyant gifts in an effort to appear more "spiritual." It was this tendency which precipitated the need for Saint Paul's letter reminding these believers of the purpose of these gifts: "To each person the manifestation of the Spirit is given for the common good . . . for the upbuilding of the church." Paul chides the Corinthians for their childish behavior and talks about building up the Church, having a constructive purpose, and making sure that everything is done "properly and in order." Instead, he wanted to see spiritual gifts bringing about real spiritual fruit and producing Christlike lives.

This is why the church promotes discernment of "charisms," or spiritual gifts. As the Catechism says:

> discernment of charisms is always necessary. No charism is exempt from being referred and submitted to the Church's shepherds. Their office is not . . . to extinguish the Spirit, but to test all things . . . so that all the diverse and complementary charisms work together "for the common good" [Catechism 801].

This discernment has enabled the gifts of the Spirit to flourish in the Church as the Spirit has raised up myriad individuals and movements to blossom forth in a full flowering of saints, communities, and ministries throughout our history.

From the day of Pentecost, God's Spirit has empowered disciples of Jesus in every generation to live a radical Gospel lifestyle and perform supernatural signs and wonders. Our generation is no exception.

## RENEWAL AND REVIVAL

As I mentioned earlier, the Catholic Charismatic Renewal movement, which has some ten million participants, represents the largest united body of Pentecostals in the world. This may not be obvious to the casual observer, since these millions are not affiliated with any one congregation or ministry. They are almost invisible, scattered like leaven in almost every normal Catholic parish, or meeting in tens or hundreds in weekly prayer groups. Only once or twice a year do thousands of us come together at a convention or conference. Then the numbers begin to look impressive.

But around the globe, God's Spirit is moving within these brothers and sisters, resulting in new communities being raised up in places like France, Germany, and Italy, where the Church seems almost dead on its feet. New communities also are being raised up in the Third World, where the Catholic Christian Church is growing with great success.

Only in America—which some call a Christian nation—are these new Catholic communities facing challenges that threaten their very existence. Many communities have been raised up by the Spirit here, but most have failed. Why? In an earlier chapter we discussed the corrosive impact of individualism, but there are other factors at work here, too.

I have witnessed spiritual renewal in Europe. There, when people are called to follow Christ, they get radical and get going. They "sell all." They join new communities. They persevere.

In America, though, it seems many try to balance following Christ with living a typical American lifestyle. Unfortunately, this has dimmed—even extinguished—spiritual renewal. People speak of radical renewal, but their lives remain unchanged. Instead of following Jesus' radical call, many instead fall for the "heresy" of nominal Christianity.

Catholic Christianity is essentially communitarian, but people prefer comfortable individualism to participating in a challenging Christian community. Perhaps this is not Catholic Christianity's time in this culture. Perhaps this culture can only endure a spirituality that is not so difficult or hard. Jesus warned that the "easy way" leads to destruction and only the "narrow way" leads to life. But many of us prefer the easy way, which does not challenge us about change, to the narrow way of the Spirit.

I pray that we all find the authentic way of the Spirit, and I am even somewhat hopeful.

If the Church and its communities persevere in America, I believe it will be due to something I call a "remnant revival." This is not a large group that fills stadiums or mega-churches, but it is real. It includes among its number many who have repented of America's paganism and national idolatry and have turned their backs on the lifestyle of the status-quo Christianity.

Will this group of true believers grow? Maybe only after the bottom drops out of our society, perhaps through a large-scale financial disaster, since money (not faith or morality) is the only thing holding American society together. Or perhaps an environmental crisis may force more people to examine the spiritual foundations of their lives.

But absent such a cataclysm, the faith of many will remain shallow and superficial, and only a small "remnant revival" will be inflamed with the love of God and empowered by God's Spirit.

## MARIAN EXTREMES?

IN ADDITION TO THE Pentecostal movement, which began in the early 1900s, this century has seen both the Jesus movement and the charismatic movement of the 1960s and 1970s. These mini-revivals brought conversion and renewal to the Church before waning in the 1980s and 1990s.

Another movement that has grown significantly during the past few decades is the Marian movement, which has become a great spiritual force in the Church. New centers of piety and devotion, such as Medugorje, have joined older Marian shrines like Fatima and Lourdes.

These sites are just a few of the places around the world where believers say Mary has appeared. Apparitions of Mary must be confirmed by the Church, and some of these apparitions are still being evaluated. But apparitions are typically accompanied by miracles and healing, prophetic messages, and calls to repentance. In all apparitions that are judged to be real, Mary calls us back to the simple Gospel of her Son, Jesus.

As with all movements, the Marian movement has its blessings and its dangers. Appearing as it did at the time that Vatican II was striving to correct extreme liberalism within the church, the Marian movement adopted a Catholic fundamentalism that some critics have jokingly described as "more Catholic than the Pope." Like fellow fundamentalists in other faiths, these true believers are convinced that they alone have God's answers and all else are in the wrong. They are exclusivistic and militant.

Marian fundamentalists often appear to be orthodox and obedient, thus they seem safe, especially to those in authority. But they take a potentially good thing too far. They are highly suspicious of fellow Catholics, believing that those who do not pray the rosary as frequently as they do are less saved. And most of them want little to do with adherents of other faiths, even though the Church has urged its members to pursue dialogue with other believers.

And there's one other problem that's even more serious. While swearing up and down that it "isn't so," many Marianists have existentially replaced Jesus with Mary as the beginning and the end, and the absolute center of the Catholic Christian faith. This is certainly not at all what Mary herself has asked for—nor has the Catholic Church, for that matter.

I recall an experience that illustrates this problem. I was visiting Jerusalem shortly after I had become a Catholic. I ran into a friend and fellow Catholic who had become very devoted to Mary. He was attempting to hand out rosaries to people on the city's streets, an act that violated the local laws. I asked him if he was telling anyone about Jesus. (Like me, he used to be an avid evangelical kid!) He responded, "No, I don't need to tell them about Jesus anymore. I tell them about Mary and let Mary tell them about Jesus!"

I also remember an incident that happened at our community, the Brothers and Sisters of Charity, when some of our members became overly zealous for the Marian movement (just as they had earlier become overly zealous for the charismatic movement). These "domestic" members, who live in their own homes and meet in small groups on a weekly or monthly basis, started to pray the rosary in conjunction with these cell groups. But soon, they wanted to transform their groups into Marian rosary prayer groups, focusing almost solely on Mary. After consulting with my bishop, I asked the group to pray the rosary before their group meetings, so they could keep the focus of their gatherings on Jesus.

Some of my comments might lead you to think I don't like the charismatic renewal or Marian movements, but in fact I consider myself a part of both. The charismatic experience opened up a whole new dynamism and power in my life. And Marian devotion has grounded me in the rich spirituality of a simple Catholic faith and life based on the centrality of the Incarnation in the bosom of the Church.

Both, however, have their dangers. I have seen these movements up close and witnessed some things that are frightening. I have seen the enemy, and sometimes he is us!

Throughout history, well-meaning individuals have attempted to put their own personal spin on Christianity and convince others to follow. That's their right, but we need to remember that any one of us can become confused or carried away. Acknowledging this once in a while helps keep us humble.

There are many movements, both positive and negative. But in the midst of it all, I am certain of this: When I look into the eyes of Jesus, I am always filled with great love, joy, and peace. When I am in communion with Jesus, I know I am coming as close as possible in this life to seeing the very face of God.

## FANATICAL FUNDAMENTALISTS AND ARCHCONSERVATIVES

WHEN I FIRST became a Catholic Christian, in February 1978, it was the extreme left-wing liberals of the church that made me uncomfortable. I had converted to Catholicism from a Protestant/fundamentalist approach that discarded many of the essentials of Catholic spirituality. I had also just emerged from a long journey through the writings of the Church fathers and monastic history, a journey that had set my heart afire with a deep appreciation of the Catholic Church and its rich and colorful history. If liberals really wanted to throw away the basics of the faith, I figured they should just come clean and admit that was what they were doing, or they should just become liberal Protestants. Why force a camel to change into a donkey, or vice versa? Isn't it better just to be a camel or a donkey (but one with deep respect for religious diversity and freedom)?

Today, though, it is the far right of the church that makes me most nervous. In reaction to the excesses of the far left, many have swung to an equally extreme and problematic position in the other direction. The fundamentals of the faith are held onto with white-knuckled determination, without a proper understanding of the history of the Church from which they came. The result is fundamentalism, but of a different kind from the Protestant version I rejected. This is hard-boiled Catholic fundamentalism.

It is obedient to the extreme forms of the faith without understanding the true Spirit and internal life of the Church from which they came. What results is an abuse of the very forms its ringleaders try to be obedient to. This is the substance of heresy itself, which is by definition a "good thing gone bad," or a good thing taken to an extreme and used badly. It betrays the good thing it was trying to protect.

In theology—as in everyday life—there's a huge distinction between "reaction" and "response" that makes all the difference. Response gets to the heart of an issue and the people involved, including oneself! Reaction is a knee-jerk action that stays stuck in externals and misses the heart—not the least of which is being stuck in our own agendas, opinions, and emotions, which in turn makes us unable to break through to our or anyone else's spirit in the Spirit of God. Reaction is rarely effective.

I am convinced that fundamentalism in all its forms is an unavoidable sociological reality with religious overtones and expressions. We see it in politics. We also see it in every major religious faith of the world. There are fundamentalist Jews, Muslims,

Christians, Hindus, and Buddhists. Now we even have fundamentalist Catholics. They are all militant and triumphalistic about their particular religious faith, to the exclusion of all others. They are angry that everyone does not share their view. And they are more than willing to use extreme attitudes, language, politics, and even physical force to protect their own exclusive domain and convert others. This has been tried by most major religions in the past, including Catholicism. It never works, but that doesn't keep some from trying it today, even though the results are dangerous indeed.

We need fundamentals but not fundamentalism. We need to conserve and "guard the rich deposit of faith" as Saint Paul exhorts Saint Timothy. But we do not benefit from archconservatism.

As I look to the immediate future of the church, I am disturbed and not a little frightened by what I see. Groups that started out as vibrant and obedient Catholics are moving farther and farther to the right into the realms of archconservatism and fundamentalism. People who used to be allies and friends are polarizing. I myself, and others like me, who have attempted to do so much to share the beauty of the Catholic Church with those who are genuinely interested in it—and to defend her against attackers—have been accused by some of not being true Catholics, of not being obedient to their extreme version of the Church. Ironically, those who have become fanatically "obedient" to the Church do a disservice to the very Church they try to protect. They go beyond the original intent of doctrines, sacraments, devotions, and authority structures, and they abuse the very teachings they try to live and share. It is dangerous to those around them. It is most tragic for the fundamentalists themselves.

We are ultimately called neither to be "right" nor "left." We are called to be "radical" in the original meaning of the word: "growing from the roots"—not "extreme," as the word later came to mean. We are not to be fanatical. An Early Church teaching, called the Didache, calls fanaticism an actual sin, because the fanatic takes an external dimension of radicalism and pushes it to an undue extreme, missing the deeper point God wants us to see.

May we be radical, not fanatical; fundamental, not fundamentalist; and conservers of the faith, not archconservatives. Then we will really be "Catholic" and "universal." Then we will really be "Christlike" and "Christian."

## TRUTH

ONE OF THE MOST important roles the Holy Spirit has in our lives is guiding us to the truth of God. God created humanity clean and pure, enabling us to hear the voice of God without effort or distortion. But through the Fall, we all went slightly off-kilter. Now the Spirit acts as an internal gyroscope, helping us know and obey God's universal truth.

In the Gospel according to Saint John, there is a strong connection between the Holy Spirit and the truth of the words of Jesus. In an amazing passage found in Chapters 14 through 16 of John's Gospel, John quotes Jesus, who calls the Holy Spirit "the Spirit of Truth." Here's what Jesus says:

> *I have told you this while I am with you. The Advocate, the holy Spirit that the Father will send in my name—he will teach you everything and remind you of all that I told you. . . .*
>
> *I have much more to tell you, but you cannot bear it now. But when he comes, the Spirit of truth, he will guide you to all truth. He will not speak on his own, but he will speak what he hears, and will declare to you the things that are coming* [JOHN 14:25, 16:12–13].

Such guidance from the Spirit was extremely important to the members of the early Church, some of whom faced extreme persecution for their faith. In Matthew's version of the Gospel, Jesus told his followers that they would be brought before "rulers and kings" to answer unjust accusations about their faith in him. He then said:

> When they hand you over, do not worry about how you are to speak or what you are to say. You will be given at that moment what you are to say. For it will not be you who speak but the Spirit of your Father speaking through you [MATTHEW 10:19, 20].

What is this truth of which Jesus speaks? It is important for us to understand that while many of the world's major religions do not believe in an absolute objective truth, Christianity does point to such a truth, and it is based on the unchanging character of God, who created the cosmos and everything in it.

Christianity teaches that concepts like right and wrong, truth and error, good and evil are not just speculative ideas concocted by theologians who live in ivory towers. Error and evil are real, and they have indisputable effects on individual and social life. They impact all areas of our lives, our relationships, and our society and culture.

When an individual knowingly behaves in a way that is in opposition to God's perfect truth, that action is called sin. The consequences of sin are never good in the long run, even though things like lying and cheating may look appealing in the short term. Sin usually does present a superficial allure. But in the long term, sin always brings hurt, injury, and destruction.

Many people today believe that good and evil are personal and relative. "What's good for you may not be good for me," they say.

But Christianity teaches that good and evil originate far beyond mere mortals.

Evil has its ultimate origin not in humanity, but in a fallen world of spirits called demons. Their chief and captain is Satan himself, the devil.

Some people picture Jesus as a conciliatory peacemaker who was full of love but never judged anyone. But that's not the picture that John paints in his Gospel. One day, Jesus was speaking of false and mean-spirited religion that opposes God's way, truth, and life. Here are the harsh words he spoke to those who followed false religion:

> *You belong to your father the devil and you willingly carry out your father's desires. He was a murderer from the beginning and does not stand in truth, because there is no truth in him. When he tells a lie, he speaks in character, because he is a liar and the father of lies. But because I speak the truth, you do not believe me. . . .*
>
> *Whoever belongs to God hears the words of God; for this reason you do not listen, because you do not belong to God* [JOHN 8:44–47].

Not even being in church protects one from the devil's seductions, as Saint Paul warned:

> *But I am afraid that, as the serpent deceived Eve by his cunning, your thoughts may be corrupted from a sincere [and pure] commitment to Christ. For if someone comes and preaches another Jesus than the one we preached, or if you receive a different spirit from the one you received or a different gospel from the one you accepted, you put up with it well enough. . . . And no won-*

*der, for even Satan masquerades as an angel of light. So it is not strange that his ministers also masquerade as ministers of righteousness. Their end will correspond to their deeds* [2 CORINTHIANS 11:3, 4, 14, 15].

Clearly, good and evil are more than mental constructs. They are a fundamental part of the universe. Jesus promised that the Spirit would guide us unto all truth, and in the next chapter, we will explore how he has fulfilled this promise.

# Attuned to the Truth

MANY CHRISTIANS SEEM TO BELIEVE THAT HOLY SCRIPTURE dropped down out of heaven, perfect and complete. According to this view, God not only directed human hands to write the Bible, but also assembled the dozens of individual Biblical books into one big volume in such a way that the central truths of Christianity would be unambiguously clear to anyone who reads it.

Unfortunately, the truth is much messier, but it's also much more beautiful, lively, and rich. Scripture came to us through a long and complex process that depended on human help within the Church—both to select the books that would be included in the Bible, and to interpret them in a way that would be both understandable and truthful.

The Catholic Church speaks of God's truth in terms of a three-legged stool. One leg is *scripture*, both Old and New Testaments, which is God's revealed truth for the human race. Another leg is *tradition*, which includes the wisdom of the Church fathers who guided the early Church and helped determine which books would be included in scripture. And the third leg of the stool is the *magisterium*, the ongoing teaching authority of the Church, which unlocks the mysteries of God's truth for us in a way that is both accurate and authoritative.

I have always seen the Catholic Church's approach to truth as similar to a rich, colorful oil painting, which has much more character and depth than a simple black-and-white line drawing. Sure, a line drawing can be true, and it can even convey something of what a person or a scene looks like. But it can't capture the subtle hues or the depth of color that can be found in the combination of oil and canvas. Catholicism's three-legged stool conveys a much more expansive notion of God's truth, which gives us more than mere objective facts—it gives us living reality.

In this chapter, we will explore each leg of the stool in depth, and perhaps after reading it you'll know more about how your own life can be guided by God's timeless truth.

## THE FIRST LEG: SCRIPTURE

IN THE OLD TESTAMENT God wrote us a letter, while in the New Testament, he paid us a personal visit in the form of his Son. Through the person of Jesus, Word was made flesh and dwelt among us. The Word was no longer a mere written word, it was incarnate. This Word was Jesus, who confirmed and fulfilled all that was written in the Old Testament.

As far as we can tell, Jesus didn't write anything that has survived the centuries. He did not write scripture; he gathered people to follow him. He did not write books; he changed lives. His emphasis was on living out God's truth while he was among us in body, soul, and spirit. He taught by example. He lived his teaching.

His mission included ideas and words, for each of us is created with a mind and a tongue to know the truth, as well as a heart to experience it and feel it. Jesus thought and felt. He preached and wept. He taught and laughed. He prayed and took action. Jesus did all of this and so much more. If he lived in our own media-saturated world, I think he would walk among us so he could personally touch us and heal us, much as he did in the Middle East two thousand years ago.

Jesus gathered a group of disciples, and from them he built an intimate community of real people committed to radically changing both themselves and the world. From among them he chose apostles—leaders who continued his ministry long after his death and Resurrection.

Like Jesus, these apostles traveled and taught, calling men and women to this new way and forming communities of faith throughout the known world, where they installed others who served as their successors. If there were questions about various aspects of Jesus' teaching or church life, the apostles had the authority to address these issues.

But after time, these early Christian leaders—and others who weren't so well known—began to communicate their ideas through a new medium that was sweeping through the Roman empire: the written word.

In the first few decades after Christ they wrote letters, or epistles. Each letter was typically sent to a particular congregation in order to settle a dispute that had arisen there. Paul wrote to the believers in Corinth—a particularly troubled congregation—about issues like division within the church and the appropriate use of spiritual gifts. Paul also wrote to the congregation at Thessalonica on the subject of the Second Coming of Christ. And he corresponded with individuals like Timothy and Titus, who were his spiritual sons and successors, and to whom he offered guidance and encouragement in ministry. Before long, churches began making copies of these letters and sharing them with other congregations, which led to the growth of a rather extensive collection of early Christian epistles.

Next, people began to write biographies of Jesus. They called these biographies the Gospels. The early Christians were eager to share their newfound faith in Jesus with the world, and writing—which had previously been available only to society's wealthiest and most educated members—was becoming one way to do that. It would be similar to someone today making a movie about Jesus, or putting his story on the Internet.

Scholars disagree about when the various gospels were written, but there are good arguments to be made that the Gospel of Mark, which was written around A.D. 50, came first. It was followed by Luke's and Matthew's Gospels, with John's being written toward the close of the century.

These four gospels are in our present-day New Testament. There were many other gospels written, too, however. One is called the Gospel of Peter, although no one is sure who actually wrote it. At least two gospels had the name Thomas attached to them. In time, there were literally dozens of "gospels" floating around the Roman world.

## THE SECOND LEG: TRADITION

THE PROBLEM WAS that not all the gospels agreed with one another. They differed on the basic facts of the story of Jesus. They disagreed about who Jesus was and what he taught, and they held opposing ideas about the purpose and nature of the Church, as well as the goals of the Christian life.

Some of these wayward gospels were little more than pious inventions by overly zealous orthodox groups. Others were diametrically opposed to the tone and teaching of the gospels written by the four apostles. Many were marked by a poverty of doctrine and thought, improbable notions, or historical irregularities of text that made it difficult to determine their actual age and origin.

Even more troubling, some gospels were clearly the work of the Gnostics, an ancient heretical sect whose members believed that both the physical universe and the human body were evil. As a result, Gnostic gospels taught that Jesus didn't really have a physical body and didn't rise bodily from the dead. Instead, he was only a ghost, or only appeared to be in the flesh. And still other gospels told fantastic tales of Jesus' infancy, portraying him as a rather mischievous child who used his magical powers at his whim.

This profusion of gospels caused confusion, but there was also a boom in epistles, most of which claimed to have been written by one of the apostles. The list of so-called epistles grew longer and longer as time went by. Some were preserved; others were lost, and we only know of these because they were mentioned in the writings of a bishop, Church father, or heretic.

Who, then, was to make sense of this growing and often contradictory collection of gospels and epistles? It couldn't be the writers, some of whom were dead. It couldn't be the laity, who were caught in the crossfire between the growing number of competing preachers, prophets, and sects. And it couldn't be the leaders of these various groups, many of whom fought among themselves as they tried to build their own spiritual empires.

The task fell to the Church's bishops, many of whom began to compile lists of which gospels and epistles were genuine, and which ones were bogus. Saint Papias (ca. A.D. 130) was one of the first to create such a list of "authoritative" gospels and epistles—or books of the Bible. These lists of books (or in Greek, *biblios*) are where we get our word for "bible."

In the first centuries of the Church, numerous bishops compiled lists that often agree in many points with the contents of our contemporary Bible. Saint Irenaeus of Lyon developed such lists in his writings against the heretic Marcion (which were written between A.D. 207 and 210), while Origen included lists in his commentaries on John and Matthew (A.D. 226–44). Others came up with lists as well, including Eusebius (in his great history of the Church, A.D. 300–325), and many more, including Saint Athanasius, Saint Cyril of Jerusalem, and Saint Augustine (A.D. 354–430).

Most of these early lists included the four gospels that most of us are familiar with, but omitted others. Also frequently included were the letters of Paul, Peter, James, and John. There were recurring doubts about Hebrews, Jude, and the Apocalypse of John, as well as The Shepherd of Hermas, the Didache, and the letters of Clement of Rome and Ignatius of Antioch. As a result, the precise contents of the Bible remained in flux for centuries until the matter was settled by a series of Church councils. These councils determined with finality the authorized list of scripture—the "canon." This word comes from the Greek word *kanon*, which means "a straight stick," and is used to mean "standard" or "rule".

This history may seem complicated, but it demonstrates an important truth: The content of the Bible (which is the first leg of our stool) was established by the authority of God through the authority of the Church (which is our second leg). Some Christians, including most Protestants, would say that this approach weakens the authority of scripture. But I would argue that it establishes its authority in an even greater way, in an incarnational way, like the authority of Jesus himself.

Scripture has always been seen in the context of the Church and the apostolic tradition from which it came. Catholic theologians often speak of sacred scripture and sacred tradition. These are not seen as two opposing truths but as two complementary currents within one stream of Divine Revelation.

Putting it another way, the Catechism of the Catholic Church, quoting the Dogmatic Constitution on Divine Revelation from Vatican II, says:

> *Sacred Tradition and Sacred Scripture, then, are bound closely together.* . . . *For both of them, flowing out of the same divine well spring, come together to form one thing and move towards the same goal.* . . .
>
> *Sacred Scripture is the speech of God* . . . *put down in writing by the breath of the Holy Spirit.* . . . *And Tradition transmits in its entirety the Word of God.* . . . *The Church* . . . *does not derive her certainty about all revealed truths from the holy Scriptures alone. Both Scripture and Tradition must be accepted.*

## THE THIRD LEG: THE MAGISTERIUM

NOW WE HAVE solved the problem of which books should be in the Bible, but we haven't yet answered the nagging question of how to interpret what the Bible says. Today, a variety of religious groups come up with different interpretations of the Bible. Let me cite just one recent example, which is admittedly extreme but which illustrates a problem that has been much more common throughout history than we might imagine.

If you'll remember, in the early 1990s a man named David Koresh ruled over a group of followers known as the Branch Davidians with his forceful personality and idiosyncratic interpretations of scripture, especially his readings of passages in the

Revelation of John about the end of the world and the seven seals. When law-enforcement officials heard Koresh talk about the seven seals, they thought he was referring to fin-footed mammals, not prophetic signs from God. This shows us how easy it is to misunderstand what scripture says.

I believe one of the best ways to understand what the Bible means is to reimmerse it in the stream of apostolic tradition. If there is a particular passage of scripture dividing the Church today (and there are many such passages), it only makes sense to go back to the early Church from which the scripture came and see if the Church fathers agreed among themselves as to what that scripture meant—and they usually did.

I strongly feel that the key to a unified understanding of scripture can be found in patristics, which is the study of the early Church fathers. As more of us Christians begin to rediscover this simple and rich stream of apostolic tradition, we begin to find ourselves coming to agreement on the Bible. We should seek to understand the Bible in the spirit of the early Church and under the inspiration of the Holy Spirit, who leads us unto all truth.

We have discussed both scripture and tradition, but what stool can stand with only two legs? The third leg on the stool of divine revelation is the teaching authority of the Church, and this authority is known as the magisterium.

In an earlier chapter we talked about apostolic succession. This discussion showed how the authority and structure of the Church were passed down from Jesus to the original apostles and then from them to their successors through the centuries. The magisterium is related to this, but is slightly different.

The term "magisterium" comes from the Latin word for one who was a "master." During the Middle Ages, the term most often referred to teachers. And Saint Thomas Aquinas used the term to refer to the teaching role of both the university professor and the Church bishop. Magisterium, therefore, means that one has the authority to teach, and when added to the previous two "legs"— scripture and tradition—this third leg provides enough balance to allow the Church to stand upright.

The experience of Saint John Henry Newman, who helped to found the Oxford Movement in England during the past century, illustrates the importance of this third leg.

Newman was meeting with a group of Anglicans (members of the English church, which broke away from the Catholic Church in the 1500s during the reign of Henry VIII) who began to rediscover the patristic roots of the Church and committed themselves to the study of both scripture and apostolic tradition. Like many people today, Newman and his group found that tradition gave them an authoritative way to interpret much of scripture, but they still had many questions.

Over time, Newman came to see that only the marriage of scripture, tradition, and the magisterium—the teaching authority of the Church, which was grounded on apostolic succession and the Petrine ministry of the bishop of Rome—gave full authority and structural unity to the Church.

Each of the world's major Christian bodies has its own approach to scripture and tradition, whether they be the most far-flung expressions of Protestantism or the closer shores of high Lutheran, liturgical Anglican, or rich Orthodox expressions of the church. Each of these expressions is, indeed, most beautiful and filled with spiritual grace in word, sacrament, and leadership. I myself find great consolation in their rich spiritual heritages and value their charism in Christ.

None of these groups, however, have achieved a full unity in Christ. Protestants are constantly divided among themselves, and new churches and denominations are regularly being launched. Even the Orthodox, whom I admire so much, still fight endlessly among themselves in sometimes hostile and violent quarrels that break the full and sweet unity of the Eucharist. They have been largely unable to mobilize even the unified of their own body into strong action that is heard throughout the world in a universal, or catholic, expression of faith beyond national, cultural, or ethnic ties. The Anglicans are perhaps more unified than the Orthodox, but even they are challenged by divisive issues such as sexuality, which separate the church's worldwide members from its more sexually permissive American members. None of these bodies has achieved the full unity that Christ spoke about.

But as Newman and others on the pilgrimage and journey toward a true spiritual home have found, the magisterium, or teaching authority, of the Catholic Church, combined with the Petrine ministry of the bishop of Rome, provides a way that brings full unity—body, mind, and spirit—to the Body of Christ, the Church of Christ.

## WISDOM OF THE FATHERS

MANY OF THE CHURCH fathers saw the importance of this unity between scripture, tradition, and magisterium. They saw this whole picture from afar, centuries before the split between Eastern and Western Christians, or the further fracturing of the West through Protestantism. They saw clearly that the scriptures could not be separated from the Church, and the Church had to be united through apostolic succession and the Petrine ministry of the bishop of Rome.

Tertullian writes with startling clarity (and perhaps a bit too much zeal) about the necessity of this theological and structural unity:

*We who walk in the rule which the churches have handed down to us from the apostles, the apostles from Christ, and Christ from God—admit that the reasonableness of our position is clear, defining as it does that heretics ought not be allowed to challenge an appeal to the Scriptures, since we, without using Scripture, prove that they have nothing to do with Scripture. . . . Not being Christian, they have acquired no right to Christian literature; and it might be justly said to them, "Who are you? . . . What are you doing with what is mine? . . . By what right do you chop at my forest? . . . By what authority? . . . This is my property. . . . I am an heir to the apostles."*

Saint Irenaeus says much the same thing in language that is just as strong but more gentle:

*The true gnosis [or knowledge] is the doctrine of the apostles and the ancient organization of the church throughout the whole world, and the manifestation of the body of Christ according to the successions of bishops, by which successions the bishops have handed down the church which is found everywhere; and the very complete tradition of the Scriptures, which have come down to us by being guarded against falsification, and which are received without addition or deletion; and reading without falsification, and a legitimate and diligent exposition according to the Scriptures, without danger and without blasphemy; and the pre- eminent gift of love, which is more precious than knowledge, more glorious than prophecy, and more honored than all the other charismatic gifts.*

I like the fact that Irenaeus declares that love, not merely knowledge or teaching abilities, is the end of all scripture, tradition, and magisterium.

Likewise, Saint Vincent of Lerns, who wrote around A.D. 450, said:

> Someone may ask, "If the canon of Scriptures be perfect . . . why is it necessary that the authority of ecclesiastical interpretation be joined to it?" Because, quite plainly, sacred Scripture by reason of its own depth, is not accepted by everyone as having the same meaning.

He then proves his point by listing various heretics—including Novatian, Arius, Pelagius, Nestorius, and many others—before continuing:

> Because of so many distortions of such various errors, it is highly necessary that the line of prophetic and apostolic interpretation be directed in accord with the norm of the ecclesiastical and Catholic meaning. In the Catholic Church . . . care must be taken [to] hold fast to that which has been believed everywhere, always and by all.

Vincent's final phrase, "that which has been believed everywhere, always and by all," has in fact become a classic statement of what it truly means to be "Catholic."

And it was the universally esteemed Saint Augustine who said, "I would not believe in the gospel myself if the authority of the Catholic Church did not influence me to do so."

It's not that the magisterium is superior to scripture. Far from it! It is the servant of scripture, whose role it is to guard and conserve the purity of both. And as we said when discussing tradition, these three legs of the stool cooperate in perfect harmony. The Catechism summarizes all of this by quoting a Vatican II document called the Dogmatic Constitution on Divine Revelation:

*It is clear, therefore, that . . . Sacred Tradition, Sacred Scripture and the Magisterium of the Church are so connected . . . that one cannot stand without the others. Working together . . . under the action of the one Holy Spirit, they all contribute effectively to the salvation of souls* [CATECHISM 95: DV10:3].

Scripture itself frequently alludes to this important balance. Listen to what Saint Paul tells his son in the faith, Saint Timothy:

*But you, remain faithful to what you have learned and believed, because you know from whom you learned it, and that from infancy you have known [the] sacred scriptures, which are capable of giving you wisdom for salvation through faith in Christ Jesus. All scripture is inspired by God and is useful for teaching, for refutation, for correction, and for training in righteousness, so that one who belongs to God may be competent, equipped for every good work* [2 TIMOTHY 3:14–17].

Saint Peter also warned against a purely "personal interpretation" of prophecy in scripture (2 PETER 1:20, 21), saying that interpretation must be made under the anointing of the same Spirit who anointed Jesus, and raised up the Church and her leaders.

Thus scripture, tradition, and the magisterium all work together in harmony as a balanced whole, with sacred scripture, apostolic tradition, and apostolic leadership all guiding the community of believers for the simple purpose of leading a more Christlike life, both individually and together as a united people.

## THE BOUNTY OF GOD'S TRUTH

WE HAVE BEEN exploring the wonders of God's truth. As we close this chapter, it is important to review briefly some of the things I find most helpful and practical about God's truth.

*It is full and final*

Scripture was given to us by God to be used privately as well as publicly. Its place is fundamental to individual piety and to public worship. Because Jesus is the "Word made flesh," and his sacrifice is "once for all," there is therefore no revelation we need to receive. The Church and the scriptures will last until the end of time as we know it.

Consequently, there is nothing else we need to receive from God in order for us to experience the fullness of salvation. In Catholic thought, there can be private inspirations and revelations to help us live the final Revelation in Christ more completely in our particular culture or time. These are subject to the discernment of the higher authority of the Church, however, which determines whether they are in harmony with the greater revelation in scripture and tradition (CATECHISM 66, 67).

*It is spiritual food*

Knowledge of scripture and its use in study and devotion is very important for everyone who is a Christian. As Saint Jerome said, "Ignorance of Scripture is ignorance of Christ." In a similar manner, the Catholic Catechism calls scripture "food for the soul" and a "font of spiritual life." We should all turn more frequently to this source of spiritual food, for it is there that we can find guidance and nourishment for our souls.

*It is reliable*

The Church teaches that scripture is divinely inspired and without theological error. As Augustine said: "It is dangerous to believe that anything in the Sacred Books is a lie. . . . For once we admit in that supreme monument of authority even one polite lie, no shred of those books will remain" (Letter to Jerome A.D. 394/95). This does not mean, however, there are absolutely no scientific or historical errors or contradictions in the Bible. The Bible is primarily a book about salvation history that includes history and science. It is first and foremost a spiritual book, not a history or science book. It is inspired and without error in everything it says in regard to God, Jesus, human nature, and the spiritual life. But to try to force it into a mold other than that which God intended for it is to do an injustice both to the Bible and to God.

We need to remember that scripture came to us incarnationally through human mediators. They did not, for the most part, take dictation from angels or the Spirit of God, as is sometimes depicted in sacred art. Their own personality and mental limitations are definitely seen in scripture, but so is the inspiration and inerrant Word of God given by the Spirit. Each biblical Gospel and each letter, as well as each Old Testament law, prophecy, or psalm, has its own unique purpose, personality, and charm. Each also carries a pure and powerful message from God to his people.

### It is understandable

The Bible is a complex book, but it is not indecipherable. Study is helpful. That is why most Catholic Bibles feature a brief introduction before each book to explain their history, authorship, and intended purpose. There are also many Bible handbooks and commentaries that can help us understand the Bible even more.

Such understanding can help keep us out of theological error. Over the centuries, many well-meaning people have gotten into serious moral and spiritual trouble by trying to read the Bible "on their own," or under the guidance of a self-proclaimed preacher or prophet. God does at times raise up such people, but he always does so within the context of the greater wisdom and balance of the Church.

I am reminded of a small group of believers in northern Indiana. They would not use doctors, believing the Bible told them to rely solely on divine healing. Their faith was admirable, but "their understanding was darkened," as Paul once said. After several women and children died in childbirth, they had to rethink their use of scripture.

After I became Catholic and discovered the book of Sirach, or Ecclesiasticus, I wished these dedicated believers had read this straightforward verse:

> Hold the physician in honor, for he is essential to you, and God it was who established his profession. . . . He who is a sinner toward his Maker will be defiant toward the doctor [SIRACH 38:1, 15].

Understanding this simple Biblical balance could have actually saved people's lives!

There are many similar verses and examples we all could cite, but the bottom line is this: Scripture properly used brings Jesus' love, joy, and peace, even in the face of life's difficulties, trials, and persecutions. A misuse of scripture, though, breeds religious fanatics and unbending fundamentalists. This makes them miserable. It makes everyone around them miserable, too.

Such misguided zeal is not God's will for his people or his scripture. God's Word does not breed quarrels and divisions. It brings the simple truth and love of Jesus, who heals and unites. It brings salvation.

*It is worthy of our veneration*

The Catechism of the Catholic Church states: "The Church has always venerated the Scriptures as she venerates the Lord's Body. She never ceases to present to the faithful the bread of life, taken from the one table of God's Word and Christ's Body" (Catechism 103; DV 21).

Every Eucharist liturgy, which is the center of public worship for a Catholic, includes not only a liturgy of the Eucharist, but first a liturgy of the Word, during which scripture is solemnly proclaimed. There can be no Mass without this proclamation of the Word of God. The bread and wine are later "confected," or transubstantiated into the Body and Blood of Christ by the Word of God spoken by the bishop or priest. The liturgy is filled with God's Word in and from scripture. Thus, the Word of God is a vital part to the liturgy. Catholics who really pray the liturgy with a listening body, soul, and spirit become men or women of the Word. They become students of the scripture in a process St. Benedict of Nursia called the "school of the Lord's service."

If we could honor and venerate God's truth in our own daily lives as the priest does during the sacred liturgy, we would experience more of the richness of God. We would truly feast on God's food for our souls.

# Liturgy:
# The People's
# Work

CATHOLIC DICTIONARIES DEFINE "LITURGY" AS "THE Church's common work," or "the work of the people of God," but words can't capture the experience that I and millions of other people have when we gather together—in groups small or large—to worship God, to hear and proclaim the Word of God, and to enter into the mystery of God through the sacraments.

If you travel around the world, you can see that there are as many different kinds of liturgies in the Church as there are different kinds of people in the world's churches. The simple monastic liturgies we have here at our hermitage have evolved over the centuries as monks have prayed together, and they are called the Divine Office, or the Liturgy of the Hours. These may include readings from the Bible, the singing of Biblical canticles or songs, lessons from Church fathers or saints, and formal prayers. But at African-American churches, the liturgy includes rollicking music, rapturous dancing, and artwork and clothing that reflect the participants' heritage. In Hawaii, liturgies can even include the hula dance.

The common denominator in all these diverse celebrations is the focus on Jesus and, in Mass or Communion services, the sacrament of the Eucharist—or Communion.

Liturgy is called the people's work because it is the most public expression of the faith and worship of the Church. Still, liturgy is also highly personal. We enter into it both individually and communally. No matter where we live or what culture we come from, liturgy actualizes and symbolizes the entirety of our faith and life in Christ. It is the public setting for worship, Word, and sacrament. And by understanding the liturgy better, we can enter into it more fully.

## GATHERING AROUND THE TABLE

IN SOME WAYS, liturgy is like a huge dining table around which the whole family gathers and upon which a complete and healthy meal is served. And in eating the meal together, the family can experience the love, joy, and peace of beautiful fellowship and community.

The family dinner table has a certain form and structure. It serves a functional role, providing us a place to gather and set our dishes. It also has a spiritual role, providing an environment for sharing, and in some cases, dinner tables are priceless heirlooms that have been passed down in the family for generations.

That's the way it is with liturgy, too. It has been assembled over thousands of years by Old and New Testament prophets, patriarchs and sages, saints, fathers and Church leaders, all of whom carefully assembled a beautiful and enduring structure out of the very best materials from scripture, tradition, and saintly experience, working under the inspiration and guidance of the Holy Spirit. Liturgy is a spiritual and ecclesiastical work of divine art.

Liturgy is also functional. It leads us into worship and praise, through which we come into God's presence. It leads us to humble repentance and forgiveness, through which we become truly ready to hear not just words but the Word of God. We hear the Word preached under the inspiration of the Spirit and the guidance of scripture, tradition, and magisterium in a way that is relevant to the here and now, calling us always to follow Christ as disciples and community. We respond to the evangelistic call of the Gospel of Jesus in the Word by professing a Catholic Christian faith that is whole and complete, radical yet balanced.

When we gather, we bring the needs of the entire Church and the whole world—from smallest to largest, least to greatest—before God in prayers, petitions, and intercessions. Some of these are voiced out loud so the whole assembly can participate knowingly. Others are only thought. Still others can only be "groaned"—beyond thought, speech, or emotion. Regardless of whether these are prayers of the tongue or meditations of profound silence, all are wrapped up in the love for God found within the community and a compassion for those outside the Church's walls.

From prayer, we move into mystery and sacrament, especially the sacrament of the Eucharist. Here, we move beyond emotions, thoughts, or words into pure mystery. We move into experience, whole and entire, body and soul, through a total breakthrough to Spirit. We incarnationally receive the Incarnation in mystery and sacrament, a union in common, a "common union" or "communion," that both includes and transcends every faculty of body, soul, and spirit. As Jesus simply IS, so this communion IS, so that we can simply BE. Be what? The Church. Disciples of Jesus. People born again.

But liturgy isn't only for us, it is for the whole world. Recent Church documents on catechesis, or teaching, tell us that worship can play a powerful role in evangelism, which is the sharing of the Christian faith with others. The new evangelization called for by Pope John Paul II (which is not really new but merely a contemporary restatement of a theology of evangelization practiced by the saints) may best be accomplished from the setting of real Christian community and Spirit-filled prayer and worship in a living liturgy. On the other hand, part of the reason that the new evangelization has not taken hold and spread in the West is that neither real Christian community nor Spirit-filled prayer and worship in liturgy are the norm in our churches. Our individualism keeps us from community. Our self-conscious pride keeps us from fully participating in the liturgy. But when community and liturgy prosper, the new evangelization will naturally blossom and spread.

All of this and so much more is included in liturgy, a public act that symbolizes our whole Christian faith. Liturgy encourages and strengthens those who believe. It calls and evangelizes those who do not. And ideally, it is the supreme action of the whole people of God. Real liturgy symbolizes and calls forth every aspect of our life in Christ as Catholic Christians.

## ALL CHRISTIANS ARE LITURGICAL

THE WORLD'S CATHOLIC, Orthodox, and Episcopal churches are all called liturgical churches because they have an intentional and historical commitment to certain fixed forms of religious ritual and common worship. But I believe that nearly all churches—Catholic or Baptist, Episcopal or Pentecostal—have a "liturgy" of one form or another, even though they may not call it that. Over time, their

repetition of routine forms of praying, singing, and worshiping together makes their meetings just as ritualistic as the services at the
Catholic or Orthodox churches down the street.

Take, for example, a typical Pentecostal or "charismatic"
church. First, there is typically a period of enthusiastic praise and
worship, possibly including the use of gifts like tongues, interpretation, prophecy, and words of wisdom. Next comes a formal message
or sermon by the leader. Then there is often a call to commitment,
followed by a period of prayer for healing, deliverance, and the outpouring of the Holy Spirit. After this comes the dismissal. On occasion, the Lord's Supper is celebrated, but probably not every
week. This, then, is the basic liturgy that is followed by thousands
of "nonliturgical" charismatic churches.

Evangelicals and mainline Protestants also have an "order of
worship." I remember it well from my Methodist upbringing and
youth. I can recall both the drudgery and the times of fulfillment
and fun in singing the ancient hymns with a pull-out-all-the-stops
organ, full choir, and four-part harmonies. I was usually moved by
the zeal of the preacher (and in some cases, bored by the lack of it!).
The preachers often impressed me by their deep faith and unshak-
able conviction about the messages they preached. I experienced
both a sense of duty and a feeling of fulfillment when I dropped my
little offering—usually a few coins—into the large collection plate
that was passed from pew to pew. Somehow, I knew my small con-
tribution would both help support the church and make possible an
outreach to the very poor in our community and around the world.
And I can still taste the rich sweetness of the grape juice that was
a regular part of our occasional communion services.

But I also recall the growing spiritual sense that something
more—something profound and mystical—was taking place in the
symbol of the Lord's Supper. Ultimately, it was a hunger for even
more of this mystical encounter that later compelled me to search

even further into the ancient roots of the early Church. It was this hunger that led me to the spiritual homeland for us all, Catholic and Protestant alike.

Nor is it only Christians who develop rituals and liturgies. It's a universal expression of our human nature, and it shows up in other religions, too, including Hinduism and Buddhism, and Taoism and Confucianism in the Far East; Judaism, Islam, and Zoroastrianism in the Middle East; and various neopagan and New Age groups throughout the West. All these believers have some sort of shared liturgy and ritual. Bowing, chanting, listening to sacred texts, and receiving something sacramental is basic to the human experience of religion. Liturgy is evident in it all. Christian or not, perhaps even religious or not, we all have a natural affinity for ritual. In this sense, human life is often liturgical.

## RITUAL NEEDN'T BE ROTE

LITURGY IS RITUAL, but ritual doesn't have to be rote. Rituals are little more than learned social actions that help us feel comfortable and safe in social settings through the use of accepted actions and words. A handshake is a ritual that is an almost automatic form of greeting in many world cultures. It serves to create a sense of openness and friendliness among strangers without requiring everyone to continually invent new ways of meeting one another, which could make many people uptight or nervous. It is human touch, but not so much as to cause embarrassment or feelings of inappropriateness. It creates communication and friendliness without extreme intimacy. A brief handshake can help break the ice when new acquaintances meet, or when workers from different departments of a company (or different regions of the world) get together for business meetings.

But as we all know, ritual can be counterproductive, even hypocritical, particularly if it gets us stuck in behavioral or emotional ruts. At these times, a little spontaneity can be good. There's nothing wrong with circumventing counterproductive social rituals that were created to make us feel safe. Sometimes we need to go beyond ritual to get through to the dangerous heart of the issue.

Liturgy is like this, too. It is a spiritual handshake, a predesigned, preordained set of behavioral guidelines about how we are to act when we gather together with one another before God. Liturgy is designed to create a sense of intimacy that is appropriate in a social setting of Christians. It draws us close, but without invading a healthy sense of privacy. After all, some people who gather in a large church setting don't really know many other people, even though these people are their brothers and sisters in Christ.

Thus, liturgy is designed to find a happy balance between the often conflicting needs for the formal and the informal, the structured and the casual, the communal and the individual, the impersonal and the personal. It puts us at ease by letting us know what comes next and what we are to do, yet it keeps us on our toes in respectful attentiveness to God and his people around us.

Things don't always turn out as planned, however, and sometimes liturgical ruts have to be broken out of, especially when a whole community is stuck in a routine that prevents its members from experiencing any real intimacy with God or one another. A rousing song or a creative homily can do this. It can also be helpful when a priest stops to explain what is happening during each part of the liturgy. Although some who have the liturgy memorized may find such explanations unnecessary, they can be a lifeline for the "liturgically impaired."

Ritual can become rote, but it's not always the liturgy itself that is at fault. Rather, it is often the spiritual attitude of the participants that needs adjustment. As the Psalmist told Hebrew worshipers thousands of years ago, we must "bring an offering and enter his courts with gladness." The offering is a readiness and willingness to offer our whole self to God—heart and mind—in and through the liturgy, even as he has given himself wholly for us in Jesus and at each mass in the Eucharist. We need to guard against letting our own responses to the liturgy become rote. Instead, we need to open ourselves to encounter God spiritually and mystically through the liturgy.

As I think about how once lively human rituals can become deadly and boring, I am reminded of how the Zen Buddhist roshi, or master, will employ a shout or a slap on the face to awaken a disciple and snap him out of his dullness. Clearly, the master's action is meant to shock and rouse his student. It is viewed as provocative or even foolish behavior, but it can bring about sudden enlightenment and a breakthrough to deeper wisdom. (I am not recommending that priests slap their parishioners! And even among devoted Zen Buddhists, such antics can be counterproductive.)

There are numerous legends about the lives of Christian saints, and from these legends we can learn a bit of how liturgy may be rightly understood and deeply enjoyed. I think of Saint Theresa of Ávila, who led her nuns in energetic dancing around the monastery chapel while she herself danced and sang in order to rediscover childlike simplicity and unaffected love. Or I think of Saint Francis, who according to his biographers was once so moved by the closeness of God that he picked up two sticks and played them like a violin, singing and dancing to his divine lover. In another instance, Francis stripped to his breeches before preaching a sermon on simplicity in one of Italy's beautiful cathedrals. On another occasion, Francis rolled down a hill through freshly fallen snow in an unpremeditated exhibition of giddy love for both the Creator and his creation.

I also recall the experience of Brother John of Alverna, a Franciscan priest who lived during the time of Saint Francis. Once, while he was celebrating Mass, he was so overwhelmed in his spirit by the reality of the words he was speaking in the sacrament he was ministering that he went into a period of ecstasy and rapture and did not come out of it until the following day. The other Franciscan friars carried John into the sacristy (a preparation room off of the main sanctuary), stood him against the wall, and waited for him to come out of his rapture.

I have also heard stories that on more than one occasion, Pope John Paul II has become so overwhelmed at what is happening during the liturgy that he has gone into a moment of silent ecstasy and rapture. Reportedly, those who were assisting him at the Mass had to tug gently on his vestments so that they might keep the service, which is sometimes attended by millions of worshipers, on schedule.

Here at Little Portion, Father Martin Wolter, O.F.M., who is my spiritual father, will often incorporate an explanation of the liturgy as we move through it, so everyone might experience it with real understanding and appreciation. Rather than serving as a disruption, this explanation of the mysteries of the Mass has helped those of us who are participating in the liturgy to enter into its reality more deeply. The narrative helps us experience greater "orthodoxy," which by definition means right praise or worship.

Perhaps we can all learn from their examples when we seek to break out of our own religious ruts.

## A FAMILY TRADITION

JUST AS A FAMILY dining table may be passed from generation to generation, the liturgies Christians use today have been passed from century to century within the family of faith from the earliest times.

The early Church was a liturgical church. The first Christian community in Jerusalem not only heard apostolic instruction, experienced charismatic signs and wonders, lived a radical common life, and evangelized their temple and city, they also devoted themselves to "the communal life, to the breaking of the bread and to the prayers" (ACTS 2:42)." Many scholars believe that this refers to both Eucharist and Liturgy.

Paul and Barnabas were prophetically called forth and apostolically commissioned with fasting, prayer, and the laying on of hands, "while they were engaged in the liturgy of the Lord and were fasting." It was actually in the context of the ritual of liturgy that "the Holy Spirit spoke to them."

Saint Paul wrote to the Corinthian Christians, chiding them for eating the Lord's Supper in an unworthy manner, and instructing them to follow the liturgical tradition he had received from God:

> For I received from the Lord what I also handed on to you, that the Lord Jesus, on the night he was handed over, took bread, and after he had given thanks, broke it and said, "This is my body that is for you. Do this in remembrance of me." In the same way also the cup, after supper, saying, "This cup is the new covenant in my blood. Do this, as often as you drink it, in remembrance of me" [1 CORINTHIANS 11:23–25].

Paul's words are still found in the Eucharistic liturgy today. Paul also laid down guidelines for order concerning the use of charismatic gifts during these public assemblies, guidelines that are still used in Catholic charismatic Masses today (1 CORINTHIANS 12–14).

Jesus participated in liturgy and ritual. He prayed the psalms with his disciples. He went up to Jerusalem to participate in the various liturgical feasts and celebrations instituted in the Old Testament. Most notably, it was in the midst of the Jewish Passover supper itself that Jesus instituted the central sacrament of the New Testament, the Eucharist. As a Jew, Jesus understood both the blessings that could come from liturgical prayer and the dangers of abusing it. But as the Messiah of the New Covenant, he entered into the liturgy of his day, transforming it and giving it a new and expanded meaning for all the people of the world. It is because of Jesus' words and actions that the Eucharist remains a sacred sacrament that plays such an important part in the public assemblies of the New Testament Church.

The early Church fathers also speak clearly of an established, yet always developing liturgy in the early Church. Saint Clement of Rome wrote:

> We ought to do in proper order all those things which the Master commanded us to perform at appointed times. He commanded the offerings and services to be celebrated, not carelessly, nor in disorder, but at fixed times and hours. He has . . . determined where and by whom He wants them to be carried out, so that all may be done in a holy manner. . . . To the high priest . . . proper ministrations are allotted, to the priest a proper place appointed. . . . The lay man is bound by the ordinances for the laity. . . . Let each of us, brethren, in his own rank, be well pleasing to God.

The Didache, a collection of teachings written in the first two centuries of the Christian era, speaks of the importance of ecclesiastical liturgies such as Confession (4:14), Baptism (7:1), fasting on Wednesdays and Fridays (8:1), the Eucharist (10:1, 9:1), and the keeping of the Sabbath on Sunday, "The Lord's Day" (14:1). Many of the rituals described in the Didache still form the basis of the liturgies used in Catholic churches around the world today.

In his "Apostolic Tradition," Saint Hippolytus of Rome paints a colorful picture of early Church liturgies around the time of A.D. 215, including the Eucharistic liturgy, Baptism, and the ordination of bishops, priests, and deacons. For me and millions of others, it is both comforting and challenging to find today's Church liturgies in the pages of these ancient Christian sources. But perhaps more than anything, seeing these ancient liturgies being practiced today creates a powerful sense of connectedness—both in Word and in Spirit—with the people and prayer of the earliest Church.

## A PINNACLE OF PIETY

LITURGY IS the highest and most public embodiment of sacred scripture, apostolic tradition, the teaching of the magisterium, and the prayers of the saints found anywhere in the life of the Church. In liturgy, these elements are woven together into a beautiful tapestry that is rich, multicolored, and strong. It is both mystical and practical, spiritual art and pastoral unity, all in one balanced and harmonious text and all centered firmly in Christ.

In this sense, the liturgy is much bigger than either the private prayer of an individual or the spontaneous prayer of an assembled group. Both private and spontaneous prayer were encouraged by Jesus and promoted by the Church, but liturgical prayer takes us to a whole other dimension of the Spirit.

Liturgy takes us beyond the particularities and peculiarities of our own personal spiritual lives to the greater reality of community, and beyond the ups and downs of our own community or location in time and space to the communion of the saints beyond space and time. Yes, we still experience inevitable ups and downs, both as individuals and as members of communities, but liturgy is a way to expand our prayer life beyond these confined and confusing human realities and break through to the eternal, infinite, and divine. From this divine perspective, we are able to have a fresh perspective on our lives, bringing God's perspective to bear on our lives and resolving the normal problems of life on earth with the divine solutions only God can bring. After we connect with God through liturgical prayer, not only do the storm waves of life settle to a more normal sea, but we are also able to guide our fragile ships through the storms so we can safely reach the harbor of heaven.

It's not just other members of the Church who are with you during the liturgy. As monks and mystics have said for centuries, God, all the angels of heaven, and the deceased saints of the Church are present with us during liturgical prayer. (We can see this teaching in the preface to "Holy, Holy, Holy" in the Eucharistic liturgy, as well as in the work of Saint Benedict of Nursia and Saint Bernard of Clairvaux.

Do we really look with our spiritual eyes to see the Spirit, the angels, and the saints surrounding us during the liturgy? Do we really believe they are present? The Church teaches that they are, and that they are also prostrate before the heavenly throne of God, enraptured in worship.

Since we are surrounded by such a chorus of heavenly worship, shouldn't we at least be willing to enter into the words, songs, and gestures of the liturgy with more than mere passive participation? For if we can begin to find God and his celestial company there, then I can guarantee that we will begin to see them elsewhere in our lives as well. Then our lives will become a liturgy and a prayer, and our spirits will become temples to house the presence of God.

## COMPLETE DEVOTION

LITURGY INCLUDES WORDS of scripture, tradition, and the magisterium, but it is also so much more. It is the thoughts of our mind, the cries of our heart, and the gestures of body as well.

During the liturgy, God involves our whole being—body, soul, and spirit—in the act of worshiping, responding to the Word, and entering into the mystery of the Sacrament. We genuflect to the Sacrament; reverently bow to the altar; make the sign of the cross; hold or lift up one another's hands; stand, sit, or kneel in reverence; and then rise from our place to go forward and receive Jesus in the Eucharist. Eastern Catholic churches even allow people to make prostrations spontaneously during the liturgy.

Furthermore, all our senses are involved in the celebration of the liturgy. The ministers and servers use holy water, incense, and candles to involve the senses of sight, smell, and touch. And in many cases, we can also view sacred art and architecture that help bring our whole being into another world while our bodies remain firmly planted in this world. Even taste is involved in the reception of Jesus under the appearance of bread and wine in the host and the cup.

Last, the act of speaking and singing the words of the liturgy brings both the tongue and the ear into the celebration. All of these actions allow the whole person to respond to the whole action of God. It is a holistic experience that we respond to holistically. It is Incarnation to incarnation, God to humanity, in and through Jesus and the Church. It is heaven already on earth, just as earth will one day return to heaven.

But liturgy does not stop there; it goes on to the mystery of transcendence. It goes beyond duality to paradox, and from paradox into complete and utter oneness. It goes from externals and internals into the pure experience of just being. This experience then transforms every other experience in life, making our lives into liturgies and our days into prayers of rebirth and enlightenment.

During the celebration of the liturgy, sight, sound, smell, taste, touch, word, and action move us from body to soul and from our physical beings to the eternal God. We move from soul to spirit in a pure intuition that is beyond sense, thought, or emotion, beyond

word or action, and even beyond meditation. It is pure contemplation. At this point, the liturgy simply is and we simply are. God is.
The liturgy, and all it symbolizes and affects, is. We are in the I AM.

This happens by moving beyond duality and paradox into complete oneness through the very words and actions of the liturgy.
We experience divinity in humanity, glory in humility, silence in
sound, word in silence, solitude in community, community in solitude, and so on.

This is not to ignore the physical realities of life. Quite the con-
trary, the transformative impact of the liturgy happens in the midst
of the very contradictions of liturgy: we find comfort even though
we may be experiencing pain or discomfort due to the bodily disciplines of kneeling, genuflecting, or bowing; we hear the heavenly
songs of God in the midst of what can sometimes be unbelievably
bad music; we hear the pure Word of God in the midst of muddled
preaching; and we experience a foretaste of the heavenly communion of saints in the midst of sometimes cold, unfriendly, and just
plain un-Christlike people.

Rather than being obstacles, these earthly realities become opportunities to transcend the limitations of the here-and-now if we
approach them with faith. Those who can participate in these spiritual transformations from the physical to the mystical will grow
more mature spiritually. But those who stay stuck in duality will remain spiritually undeveloped and immature.

But when we allow the liturgy to help us break through to God
and the infinite, we begin to experience every sense, every action,
every sound, every thought, every emotion, every concept, and
every form in a whole new way. All these things become breakthroughs to Infinity and the Eternal, and they allow us to hear with
open ears the original music of God.

Every genuflection or bow becomes an act of enlightenment
and rebirth. Every sound and word becomes a sound beyond con-

cept or form. Every sight and smell is beyond any discrimination or description. Every taste and touch is the taste and touch of the Infinite and Eternal. Each experience is savored but not possessed, fully appreciated but with dispassion and detachment. Liturgy, Word, and Sacrament become an experience of the highest state of contemplation beyond all knowledge. It is the known in unknowing, a light seen only in darkness. It is beyond all words or knowledge, but for those who have experienced it, it is the most reality, it is wisdom, it is God.

But this is no walk in the dark. Through the liturgy, the subjective is grounded and directed by the objective. Unknowing is based on knowing. This kind of experience doesn't make us "so heavenly-minded that we are no earthly good." The eyes or the mind do not grow blank. The emotions do not shut down. The body does not grow weak. These are all signs of false contemplation and delusion, usually based on a desire to do all this without proper guidance or direction. The rapture and ecstasy of the Christian mystic is not the same thing as mental drifting or "blissing out." Such false expressions can be dangerous and destructive.

Real contemplation makes us more aware of ourselves and the people and world around us. The body becomes sensitized to almost athletic efficiency in the service of the soul and the spirit. The whole of the human being fulfills its original divine call and purpose.

It's impossible for an external observer to completely tell what is happening within a person's spirit during the celebration of the liturgy. But I know that as I kneel and bow, make the sign of the cross, stand or sit, sing or speak, or even be quiet, a whole other world of wonder, enlightenment, and rebirth is going on inside.

One does these things reverently and fully, and never for demonstration or show. In fact, when I really find this mystical dimension in liturgy, I become detached from myself, or from enlightenment itself. I am more aware, but unaware of the awareness, because God IS and is ALL. Through liturgy we can discover the greatest Being of all and become one in him.

## ENJOY THE JOURNEY

WE CAN LEARN a lesson about celebrating the liturgy from Zen Buddhist monks who find "satori," or "enlightenment," in the very acts of their own rituals. For example, these monks place so much importance on ritual acts that they call them "bowing practice," "chanting practice," "listening practice," and so on, indicating that the actions themselves are important parts of the process. And the Buddhist tea ceremony, which is both an action and a contemplative experience, takes on a near-sacramental importance.

We can also learn about liturgy from a simple image. Picture a car driving down California's Highway 1, which snakes along the western edge of the American continent. Or if you like, picture a car passing through the Smoky Mountains, or perhaps crossing the Continental Divide in Colorado. Wherever it is you picture the car, look inside the passenger compartment to see the driver—who is looking out the windshield with a mixture of amazement and awe. Then, seated next to the driver in the passenger seat is a person who is totally oblivious to the majestic natural beauty passing by outside the little compartment. Instead, this passenger is looking at a road map!

The words and rules of the liturgy are only a map, signposts along the journey. And in a sense, even liturgy itself is only a map or sign. But none of the things—the words or the act of the liturgy itself—are to be confused with the journey. Sure, it is important to read the map and follow the signs. Without them, you can get terribly lost. But reading the map isn't as important as taking—and enjoying—the journey.

Some people spend all their time with their nose in a map. They look at road signs but miss the majesty. They want to arrive at the destination, but they're so uptight that they almost never enjoy the journey. And by the time they arrive, they're a nervous wreck, and they have made their traveling companions nervous wrecks as well.

How much better it would be to balance a proper attentiveness to maps and signs with an alert attentiveness to the wonders of the journey. Look out the window at the beautiful countryside, the rolling hills, the abundant fields and farms, the cities and towns, the children and the families. The wonder of life itself is there to behold all along the way. And when you arrive at your destination, you'll be welcomed warmly by family and friends and invited inside to loving and lively conversation around a table laid out with good food and drink, with a sweet dessert as well!

So should it be for us at liturgy. Enjoy the journey. Have a good visit. Sit as friends and family around the table of the Lord, and commune together in God's richest food and fare. Don't get stuck in the maps and the road signs. You'll only make yourself and everyone else miserable. Pray the liturgy rightly, enjoy this wonderful blessing from God, and be a blessing to all.

# The Holy Mystery of Sacrament

THROUGH THE CENTURIES, SAINTS, MYSTICS, AND WISE men and women have described the Christian life as a love relationship between God and humanity. When God made us, he didn't produce preprogrammed robots who would automatically obey every command. Instead we were given tremendous freedom, and few things please God as much as when we voluntarily enter into a love relationship with him. Love is a decision, but love still goes beyond mere logic to mystery.

Sacrament represents an essential dimension of our love relationship with God, and it plays an important role in forming intimate unions with our human brothers and sisters. Just as a man and a woman who desire to be married participate in a wedding ceremony where they affirm and publicly express their vows, the sacraments of the Church give us opportunities to experience the sacred mysteries of God with our entire person: body, soul, and spirit. Today, Eastern Orthodox and Catholic Eastern Rite churches still speak of sacrament as "a holy mystery." Latin Rite Catholics do the same.

In the earlier chapters of this book, we moved from Spirit to Word, and from Word to liturgy. Now, as we come to the close of the book, we move effortlessly from liturgy to sacrament. A similar movement from Spirit to Word to liturgy occurs in private mystical prayer, as well as in communal celebrations.

Our English word for sacrament comes from the Greek word for mystery, and from the Latin words for oath or pledge. To participate in sacrament represents the culmination of our love relationship with Jesus. Beginning with the first mystical spark that drew us to God, we have moved on to a dialogue with God through prayer and hearing the Word of God. Following this dialogue with God, we have experienced moments of breakthrough and connection on a deeper spiritual level. As our marriage with God has grown and deepened, we have experienced a spiritual consummation through an experience of God's Spirit that is beyond words. Attraction, dialogue, and commitment have allowed us to break through the barriers that separate us from God and to experience him in body, soul, and spirit.

In communion with our divine spouse, we have entered into a naked embrace that places complete trust in the other's character, intentions, and commitment to us. We hold nothing back for self, but empty all we are in ourselves for the sake of the other. This is the place of sacrament. This is the place of mystery. Yet this love relationship with God is a mystery that speaks of a much deeper reality than mere words or thoughts. It is the heart of the mystery of love.

Poets have long proclaimed that human love is a mystery. No one really knows why two people fall in love. There are companies that rely on detailed, computerized surveys to find matches for men and women seeking partners. But just because computers predict that two people will be perfect for each other, this doesn't mean they will fall in love. Some will hit it off right away, while others won't, and nobody really knows why. The true nature of the spark that ignites a romance that grows into a love is a mystery. It is sacramental.

On the other hand, love is a decision that incorporates and directs our emotions but is also based on objective truths. Often two people are attracted to each other with the help of such objective factors as common interests, similar backgrounds, shared views on deeply held values and beliefs, and similar goals for the future.

If these objective truths don't line up, it's difficult for two people to establish a deep and long-lasting love relationship, even if there was a spark of romance at the beginning. When he wants to live at the North Pole, and she wants to live in the Bahamas, true love is difficult, if not impossible. Even though there was an initial attraction, marriage might not be such a good idea when there are serious objective disagreements about important issues. For a marriage to grow and blossom, it must effectively incorporate the realities of fact and feeling, heartfelt emotions and deeply held convictions.

Jesus once said, "For where your treasure is, there also will your heart be" (MATTHEW 6:21). He was telling his hearers that if they would truly treasure the will of God, their hearts would surely follow. It is the same with human love. Love is an act of the will combining the objective truth of the mind and the subjective emotions of the heart in a union of will and feeling, truth and love.

When this harmonious combination exists, a marriage can be initiated in love, witnessed in a formal act of commitment, and consummated in a full union of body, soul, and spirit. Such a union transcends truth or emotion and reaches the heights of mystical union. It incorporates body, soul, and spirit but goes beyond them all, creating a union that is beyond all duality, and enlightening all in mystery.

## SACRAMENTAL REALITY

FOR THE CATHOLIC Christian, all of life can be an experience of sacrament. Nature is sacramental in that it reflects the handiwork of the Creator. Through the eyes of faith, everything that is is an expression of the invisible attributes of God.

More directly, the Church—which is both physical and spiritual—is a universal sacrament of salvation. And Jesus is our sacrament par excellence. He is both incarnate and transcendent, objectively true and mysterious. Together, Jesus and the Church open the door so that we can experience the sacramental mysteries of God. They are both truth and life, ancient and timeless, truth and Spirit, theology and song.

When most people speak of sacraments, however, they refer to the specific ritual elements that have been recognized from the time of the ancient and apostolic churches of the early centuries down to our own day.

The Roman Catholic Church recognizes seven sacraments: Baptism, Confirmation, the Eucharist, Penance, Matrimony, Holy Orders, and Anointing of the Sick. Not all Christian bodies agree on this precise number. Protestants, for example, identify only two sacraments, Baptism and the Eucharist, which is called The Lord's Supper. But all Christian churches observe these sacramental traditions, even though they may not call them sacraments.

There is widespread agreement among the majority of the world's Catholic, Orthodox, and Anglican believers that sacraments are an external, physical sign or symbol of God's grace that also effects, or causes, grace. Most Protestants would disagree, saying that the sacraments are only outward signs or symbols of a grace that already exists through faith. For Catholics, that's a good definition as far as it goes, but it doesn't go far enough. For Catholics, sacraments both symbolize grace and also help that grace grow stronger. How grace does so is part of the mystery of the sacraments.

A sacrament is like a kiss between husband and wife. It symbolizes a love that exists already, but it also causes that love to grow stronger. It is sacramental and mysterious. So it is with the seven sacraments:

*Initiation*

The Church teaches that Baptism, Confirmation, and the Eucharist are sacraments of initiation. That means these are rituals enjoyed by new Catholics which symbolize and effect the believer's desire to grow in a love relationship with God. It is also said that all sacraments of the Christian experience flow out of the primary experience of Baptism, which powerfully symbolizes the believer's dying to self and rising again to new life in Jesus.

*Daily*

The Eucharist is also considered an ongoing sacrament: one that is a continuing part of the believer's regular relationship with God. Penance is the other ongoing sacrament.

*Vocational*

There are two vocational sacraments, which symbolize and effect one's sense of calling and commitment to follow a new way of life. These two vocations are Marriage and Holy Orders (or Ordination).

*Healing*

And finally, the sacrament of Anointing of the Sick is part of the Church's ministry of compassion to the seriously sick or the dying.

There is so much I would like to say about each of these sacraments, but for now I will focus on the Eucharist, which plays such a central role in the believer's ongoing love relationship with God and provides us with such a powerful illustration of how sacrament opens the door for us to go from body and soul to spirit.

## GATHERING FOR THE EUCHARIST

LET ME USE the example of a Eucharistic service at the Chapel of Charity from the Little Portion Hermitage, which is the motherhouse of my community, the Brothers and Sisters of Charity.

Our chapel is set up "monastic-style," with the lectern for the Word of God in the scriptures at one end, and the altar for the celebration of the sacramental incarnate Word of God, the Eucharist, at the other. When we enter the Charity Chapel, we first dip our finger in the holy water font and make the sign of the cross, as a remembrance of the beginning commitment we made to Christ and the Church through Baptism. This is a renewal of our Baptismal promises at the beginning of our liturgical service, or of every private prayer time, within the chapel.

Next, we genuflect to the whole mystical, incarnate Word of our faith in the reserved Sacrament in the tabernacle. We also do a deep reverent bow to the altar, upon which the Eucharist will be confected through the Word of God spoken by the bishop or his

priest. By confection we mean that it is changed from the simple elements of bread and wine into the real presence of the body and
blood of Christ, mystically, under the appearance of bread and wine.

Our seats are set up facing one another around this axis, with
the Word of God at one end in the lectern and the sacrament at the
other in the altar and the tabernacle. So the community gathers
around these two primary realities of Word and Sacrament every
time we pray publicly as community.

The typical monastic Mass in our community begins with a song
of praise, or a hymn, followed by the monastic chanting of the
Psalms in the Divine Office. This Divine Office comes from a long
tradition combining the monastic practice of praying the Psalms in
private and the public and corporate recitation and then singing of
the Psalms in the cathedral tradition, which goes back to the cathedrals of the early Church. The Psalms cover a wide variety of top-
ics, from praise to complaint, from exaltation to repentance, from
almost delirious joy to the depths of despair. They are intended to
represent the wide spectrum of the human response to our infinite
God—body, soul, and spirit—including gestures, emotions,
thoughts, and yes, a breakthrough to the infinite, the eternal, and
the intuitional in the Spirit.

At this point, the priest may elect either to use the Divine
Office as the Penitential Rite, or to move into a more formal
Penitential Rite with the inclusion of the Kyrie, a Greek word representing an invitation of "Lord have mercy, Christ have mercy,
and Lord have mercy," followed by a formal absolution of sin by the
priest or the bishop of the Church. In this we admit our common
humanity, frailty, and sin—"missing the mark of total perfection
and balance." Next comes the Confiteor, which is a recited prayer
admitting our sin in thought, word, and action through either com-
mission or omission, and invoking the intercessory prayer of the

whole Church Catholic, along with all the angels of Heaven and, in particular, with the believing community with which we live, so that we might receive the fullness of forgiveness in Jesus, and the fullness of the empowerment of the Holy Spirit, that we might be strengthened so as to grow out of these patterns of sin in our life.

This Penitential Rite helps to clear the path or the way of any obstacles keeping us from reaching our desired destination in and through our public celebration of word and sacrament. It clears the mind and emotions from any distractions or from a lingering sense of guilt before we hear the wonderful Word of God or enter into the deepest mystery of God in the Eucharist.

We next enter into the Liturgy of the Word using the lectern at the entrance of the chapel and the altar at the end of the chapel, so the Liturgy of the Word of God precedes the Liturgy of the Eucharist, in order for the sacrament to be legitimate and full. As Liturgy precedes the Sacrament, the Word of God precedes and confects the Eucharist. It is, as it were, a journey from the objective and the subjective into the mystical, from thought and emotions into intuition, from soul and body into pure spirit.

With the Liturgy of the Word, we listen to its proclamation with our mind and allow it to sink deep into the heart and into emotions. Then we are ready to make the journey past thought and emotion, past body and soul into pure mystery and intuition, yet in a way that does not leave behind body and soul, thought or emotion, but in fact includes and transforms them into the primacy of spirit and intuition, back to the original plan of God for each individual human being, for the whole human race, and yes, reaching out to the end of creation with this wonderful rebirth and enlightenment and transfiguring transubstantiation.

As with Liturgy, the proclamation of the Word is not simply a proclamation of the scriptures. It is a proclamation of apostolic tradition and scripture as interpreted by the magisterium of the Church, to ensure maximum fullness and balanced equilibrium, in a way that will bring true harmony, prosperity, and life to each and every listener, and to the community gathered as a people of God.

We can't find the canon, or the truthful yardstick of scripture, in scripture alone, nor in our idolatry of a particular powerful teacher or unusually charismatic preacher. It is only when we rec-ognize the full authority of the apostolic tradition and magisterium that the wonderful gifts of the Spirit will be poured forth upon teachers and preachers, both clerical and lay, of the whole Church.

Of course we invoke that same power of the Spirit upon the proclaimer of the Word, the preacher of the Word, and upon all who listen. Without that anointing of the Spirit, the Word of God cannot be properly heard in a way that brings true spiritual life. I am reminded of the quote of Saint Bonaventure in the thirteenth cen-tury, at the beginning of his Breviloquium, or his brief treatment of the Roman Catholic Church, where he says that without the Spirit of God, the Word of God cannot be properly heard or understood, because it was in that Spirit that the scriptures themselves were both written and compiled.

I am also reminded of the quote of Saint Bernardine of Siena, the great fifteenth-century reformer of the Franciscan movement. He said that if one had to choose between the celebration of the sacraments without the Word of God, "which is liturgically im-proper and impossible," and hearing the proclamation and preach-ing of the Word of God without the sacrament, one should choose the preaching of the Word of God.

It is interesting to note that the early Franciscans did preaching tours where they would preach to anywhere from thirty thousand to fifty thousand people at a time in the big piazzas, and lawns out in front of the major basilicas and cathedrals of the churches of

Italy and southern Europe. The preaching itself would go on for three or four hours at a time, with the crowd circulating around in front of the platform, since that many people could not hear an unamplified voice, and with the friars holding up large banners in which the subject of the sermon was portrayed in pictures and in art. After this preaching, the friars would lead the crowd into the major church and the small churches of the area, for the celebration of the Eucharist.

From the Liturgy of the Word, we move into the Liturgy of the Eucharist, our deepest mystery. The Liturgy itself is composed of scripture and the ancient prayers of Catholic Christianity. They are indeed very beautiful, and even poetic, if not greatly mystical. It is during this Liturgy of the Eucharist that the ordained minister of the Church representing apostolic succession, and the faculties granted with or from the local bishop, first invokes the power of the Holy Spirit over the elements, in the Epiclesis, within the Eucharistic Prayer, and then with word and gesture, and the power of his office, confects the Eucharist, changing the simple elements of bread and wine into the real presence of Jesus, body and blood, under the appearance of bread and wine.

This is the fullness of sign, symbol, and sacrament. All that is Church is represented in this ineffable coming together of every aspect of the faith. The priest is there, who represents the whole of the Christian community to God, and the whole of Jesus to the Christian community. The gesture is there, representing that Jesus came in the flesh and that he saves us full and entire, inclusive, not only in spirit, but also our body. The Word is there, representing not just a written word, not just a vaguely interpretive apostolic tradition, but its fullness, scripture, and tradition and the magisterium of the Church. The Church is there, in the priest or bishop, who represents not only Christ and the fullness of the Church but the apostles of the Church as well, the fullness of apostolic succession, and in the case of Roman Catholics, the Petrine ministry of Saint Peter and his successors as primary among all the bishops and Vicar of Christ.

Finally, and most important, incarnation of the living Word of God is there, sacramentally. Jesus continues his incarnation in and through the things of creation in this bread and wine. Creation is reconciled to Creator, and Creator is manifested in and through Creation. The bread and wine representing all of the work of human flesh—as both the basic fruit of our labor and the food of our body—represents humanity transformed in the presence of the Deity. The Deity taking on humanity, and through this wonderful mystery of humanity and divinity breaking through to the mystery of complete divinity beyond words.

Some would ask, "Why bread and wine? And why not another person, or group of people?" First, the Church herself is the great sacrament of salvation, even as Jesus himself was and is the sacrament par excellence. But since the Church is made up of sinners, and Jesus was not a sinner, we represent not only the perfection of God but the sinfulness of humankind as well.

In finding a perfect sacramental symbol and presence, the Lord utilized bread and wine. These are two powerful symbols of humanity's quest for survival as well as our creativity and productivity. These symbols are essentially neutral. By that I mean that they do not in themselves speak of righteousness or sin. Therefore, they remind us of Jesus, who was fully human, even in the midst of his divinity. He was human without the presence of sin.

Those of us who receive Communion must do this holistically—body, soul, and spirit. In Catholic churches, at the time of Communion, we rise up from our seat and go forward in a Communion line. This is a wonderful symbol of continuing conversion and growth in Christ. One must rise up from where one is in one's life and go forward to meet Christ. We must be willing and ready to go forward, to not stay stuck in the habits and the problems of where we are in life.

Jesus loves us enough to meet us where we are, as we sit and participate in the liturgy, but he also loves us enough to call us forward, and to call us to change, to keep growing in him. We go forward, both individually and communally. Each individual must take his or her own place in the Communion line, but we do form one group, one community, going forward together to experience the full reception and the manifestation of the mystery of Christ, the Holy Eucharist. While we go forward, we pray in silence, or we sing the Communion hymn. We are encouraged by one another, those who have already received, or those who have yet to receive, or even those who for whatever reason will not receive on this particular day.

To continue our journey in Christ, the journey is not made alone, or without the wonderful power of worship and prayer as individuals, and as a community. Finally, we stand before the bishop, priest, or deacon, or the lay minister of the Eucharist. Before receiving Communion, some make a reverent bow and a sign of the cross. Some will receive reverently within their open and naked hands, the left hand resting gently but firmly upon the right, or upon the tongue, as has been done for many years in the Western Church. Both are symbols of great childlikeness and humility. The open hands, a symbol of nakedness, emptiness, and poverty. You cannot hold anything else while opening yourself to this mystical or sacramental experience of Jesus.

We must let go of all to receive he who is the author of all and in fact is all. We are overwhelmed as we receive a Creator within the palm of our own hands. He who is so great because he is willing to be so vulnerable for our salvation. He who is the author of all, being held within the palm of the hand of his own creation.

This is a great wonder of the condescension of love, the willingness to become the smallest of the small, even though one is the greatest of the great, in order to bring salvation to all, both the small and the great in our midst.

Those who receive upon the tongue manifest this humility in the face of this great wonder by saying that they are not even willing to dare to hold in the palm of their own hands the King of kings and Lord of lords. No, they would rather allow those to whom the ministry has been specifically given, through apostolic succession in the bishops, and those who have received faculties from him, to distribute Communion directly upon their tongue, without their intervention, their misinterpretation, or their miscalculation of the beauty and perfection of this sacrament. It is a humbling thing to stand before another human being, extending one's tongue, even as a babe waiting to be fed by its mother, mother Church. The experience is like that of a chick being fed by the mother bird. It is a statement of total poverty and vulnerability before the minister of the Church, and yes, most important, before God himself. It is the ultimate expression of vulnerability in the place of he who became so vulnerable for us, so that we might be brought back to the full strength of the original plan of God for all of humanity.

After receiving Communion we go back to our seats, to the places in life from which we all came and to which we all must go back. We sit together, yet very much in privacy, in the solitude of our own emotions, thoughts, and spiritual intuitions. At this point the Church recommends that liturgy be minimized, in terms of action, words, songs, or gesture. The ideal liturgy at this moment is silence. The ideal communal experience is solitude together. After having received the greatest mystery, the Sacrament, we enter into a place that is beyond words, beyond emotions, beyond ideas, thoughts, or forms, beyond action. It is ultimate action in stillness, ultimate word in silence, ultimate emotion in pure spiritual intuition. It is simply being with he who is. As the saints have said, at this moment, we are simply with he who is. We simply be together. We are one. This moment is not to be rushed, or prematurely ended. It is to be given great space and time, so that Jesus might speak his word beyond all words, within the fullness of our being with the fullness of his being.

After an appropriate space and time for reflection after Communion, the people begin moving out of this deep silence, stillness and communal solitude, back into the world of words, and sometimes frenetic activity and sociological responsibility in family, church, and work in the world. In charismatic churches, this is often preceded by a time for word gifts or healing ministry. Here we move out from the pure contemplative state into a ministerial state, albeit still within the realm of the very personal and intimate. After this time, many churches will move to the more functional aspects of the Church and local civil community by way of announcements. These sometimes seem a bit schizophrenic after the very personal and intimate things we have just experienced, but they are really a natural outgrowth and progression from the deep mystery of the Eucharist into the functional realities of life. It is, in fact, there that the new evangelization, the sharing of the Gospel of Jesus Christ through all that we are, takes place in the most tangible ways.

Following the announcements come the final prayer and blessing over the congregation, and yes, the final song of celebration, joy, and sending out. This last song is not just something to get the recession down the aisle, or to get the community out of the church. It is a sending forth into the world with great enthusiasm and joy. After we have worshiped God, turned from our sins, heard the powerful preaching of the Word of God, and received the deepest mystery of the sacrament, we take of that whole experience of Jesus back out into a world that so desperately needs him.

Thus we can see from the layout of our little chapel, and the structure of the liturgy itself, the fullness of our corporate, our communal walk with Christ. These same steps are experienced on an individual basis and on a local communal level in monastic community, and in the mystical tradition of the saints. What is true of the whole body of Christ is also true for each individual in Christ, and what occurs with the whole universal Christian community, or Catholic Christian Church, is also true of each of the communities and movements and families within the Church.

## THE DOORWAY TO GOD

SACRAMENT ISN'T AN END in itself but a doorway into a deeper and fuller experience of God on a daily basis. There is a youth organization within the church who I have worked with many times over the years, and I think they get it right when they say, "The Mass never ends; it must be lived."

When rightly understood, liturgy and sacrament turn all of life into liturgy and sacrament, and every moment can become an opening to the eternal. If we hear the Word of God correctly during Mass, every word we hear or speak can become holy and sacred. If we receive the Eucharist rightly, every source of bodily nourishment can become a heavenly nourishment from God, and our whole life can become nourishment from God for others.

Sacrament is not only something we celebrate at a particular place at a particular time, it is a whole way of life that is mystically supported by our regular celebration of the Eucharist in our own particular place and time.

Of course, this is just a preliminary introduction to the sacramental richness of the Church. There is so much more to tell. There are so many more rooms in the house of God. Over the centuries, the Church has created an extensive mystical theology to guide our deeper relationship with God, as well as a broad-based social theology to guide our moral and ethical behavior in the world.

At least we have made a beginning. I have tried to show you some of the rooms in the house. Come on in. Take a look around. I believe you will find your home here.

## ABOUT THE
## LITTLE PORTION HERMITAGE

FOUNDED IN 1980 AND LOCATED OUTSIDE OF EUREKA Springs, Arkansas, Little Portion is the monastic motherhouse of the Brothers and Sisters of Charity, a Franciscan-based community including celibates, families, and singles, and supporting a network of people living in their own homes in America and five other countries. If you would like more information, please request our brochure, which describes our community and values.

We also run a conference center, Little Portion Retreat and Training Center at MORE Mountain, which offers regular retreats and workshops on contemplative prayer, simple living, monastic traditions, mystical prayer, and other subjects. Contact us if you're interested in videos or tapes from past conferences, or for a schedule of upcoming events.

We also publish a newsletter that includes news and information about our community and schedules of upcoming events at our conference center, as well as a schedule of my performances around the country, information on ordering books and music, a list of products made here at Little Portion and sold to support our ministries, and articles of interest. We would be glad to add you to our mailing list.

You can contact us by the following means:

- You can write us at: ROUTE 7, BOX 608, EUREKA SPRINGS, AR 72632
- You can phone us at: (501) 253-7710
- You can e-mail us at: HERMITAGE@ARKANSAS.NET
- Or you can visit our home page at the following Internet address: HTTP://WWW.JOHN-MICHAEL-TALBOT.ORG

JOHN MICHAEL TALBOT is a musician, teacher, and writer who practices the Franciscan traditions. His albums have sold more than four million copies, and he is the author of thirteen previous books, including *The Lessons of St. Francis, The Lover and the Beloved: A Way of Franciscan Prayer,* and *Meditations from Solitude.*

Intrigued by the life of Saint Francis of Assisi, which prompted an interest in the Catholic Church, he began studying at a Franciscan retreat center in Indianapolis, joining the Secular Franciscans in 1978. Then in 1980 he founded an integrated monastic community located in Eureka Springs, Arkansas, based on the Franciscan principles of simplicity and self-sufficiency.

Today his community, the Brothers and Sisters of Charity, has about thirty-seven members in Arkansas and another five hundred worldwide. The Brothers and Sisters of Charity is the only community of its kind in North America with canonical status from the Catholic Church. The work of the Brothers and Sisters of Charity includes providing assistance to nearly anyone in need.

# John Michael Talbot
## cave of the Heart

With the release of *Cave of the Heart*, John Michael Talbot revisits his musical roots. For over twenty years, John Michael has created music that ministers to the Mind, Body, and Spirit. With more than three million tapes and CD's sold, he has been a consistent bestseller in Contemporary Christian Music.

*Cave of the Heart* returns to the original sounds of John Michael—aggressive virtuoso guitar-playing, tight vocal harmonies, and lyrics and melodies that reach into your soul. Many have compared his early albums to the sounds of Crosby, Stills, Nash and Young; the Eagles; and Dan Folgelberg. With "Cave," the listener will enjoy reaching back to the past for a sound that captures John Michael Talbot's roots, intertwined with the sounds and melodies that will captivate your heart.

John Michael plays a steel string guitar given to him by Michael Card, and the result is a vintage sound that built the foundations of Contemporary Christian Music. Michael Card, Phil Keaggy, and Bonnie King joined John Michael in the studio for this recording—the results are electrifying.

*Cave of the Heart* flowed easily out of the writings from *The Music of Creation*. This recording will allow readers to better understand how the music and lyrics of John Michael are part of this "Creation."

Available August 1999 at Bookstores, Record Retailers, and Christian Bookstores everywhere.

"Visit www.caveoftheheart.com to preview the album."